A FAMILY

ORNELLA & PIETRO PISANO

KUYPERS-SCHUSTER FAMILY

HAUN CLARKSON & PAUL BREWSTER

NICKY BUTLER

GEORGE & DIANA SHARP

CREATIVE
spaces

GERALDINE JAMES

CREATIVE
spaces

INSPIRED HOMES AND CREATIVE INTERIORS

CICO BOOKS
LONDON NEW YORK

Published in 2013 by CICO Books
An imprint of Ryland Peters and Small
20-21 Jockey's Fields   519 Broadway
London   5th Floor
WC1R 4BW   New York NY 10012

www.rylandpeters.com

10 9 8 7 6 5 4 3 2 1

Text © Geraldine James 2013
Design and photography copyright
© Cico Books 2013

A CIP catalog record for this book is
available from the Library of Congress
and the British Library.

ISBN: 978 1 78249 055 5

Printed in China

Project Editor: Gillian Haslam
Contributing Editor: Helen Ridge
Designer: Paul Tilby
Photography: Andrew Wood

For digital editions visit
www.cicobooks.com/apps.php

Without question, we all enjoy looking into other people's homes. Observing the design and decorating choices made by others offers an intriguing insight into what makes them tick and what their priorities are. In my previous books, I have taken bite-size snapshots of walls and displays but here I wanted to show entire homes, revealing how the owners and their families live, and how they relax and entertain.

Featured here are diverse and fabulously unique homes, such as the magical Fornasetti house and archive in central Milan, two Brooklyn brownstones, and a modernist "Space House" in the middle of the English countryside. IN SPITE OF THE DIVERSITY, THERE IS A COMMON THREAD THAT CONNECTS THEM ALL—EACH OF THE OWNERS INHABITS A CREATIVE WORLD OF ONE SORT OR ANOTHER, FROM FASHION AND PHOTOGRAPHY TO ART AND ARCHITECTURE. What's more, they all know exactly how they want their homes to be and how they wish to live. There are no slavish followers of fashion here, simply people who trust their instincts to do exactly what feels right for them. I am proud to count many of them as long-standing friends, and I am incredibly grateful to everyone involved for being so gracious and welcoming.

The home is the heart of most people's lives, offering respite from the frantic and challenging world outside. It is the place where we can truly unwind and refocus. For that simple reason, it is vital that nothing about it jars the senses or challenges the eye. It has to be cocoon-like and pleasing. For some that will mean an abundance of soft furnishings and cozy chairs, but for others, such as me,

◄◄ An artist's test board leans against the wall in John Derian's apartment, creating an unconventional piece of unique art. The lampstand just in front of it was created from a piece of wood salvaged from old furniture. Smart upholstered chairs add a touch of comfort.

it means being well ordered and tidy before I can even think about relaxing. That part of my personality, as well as my taste and style, are reflected in how I have decorated my home.

Although we are happy to be exposed to new and thought-provoking ideas through the media and retail, HOW WE FURNISH, DECORATE, AND STYLE OUR HOMES SHOULD BE INDEPENDENT DECISIONS THAT WE MAKE TO SUIT OUR LIFESTYLE AND NOBODY ELSE'S. THERE WAS A TIME WHEN WE ALL FELT OBLIGED TO LIVE IN SIMILARLY SIZED AND SHAPED HOMES, BUT THE OPPOSITE IS NOW TRUE. Here, we feature the family home created from part of a Victorian school, and the fantastically original open-plan apartment that was originally one floor of an old garment factory. Non-conformity is no longer frowned upon, and the more unusual and individual a home, the better. We love the raw, the rough, and the recycled, such as a water tank used as a bedside table and a collection of pockmarked mirrors forming a decorative wall display.

EACH AND EVERY ONE OF US HAS A CREATIVE SIDE, WHICH WE MUST TAKE CARE TO NURTURE, AND OUR HOME IS THE ONE PLACE WHERE WE CAN TRULY EXPRESS OURSELVES. USE THIS BOOK TO OPEN YOUR MIND TO IDEAS AND ALTERNATIVE WAYS OF DOING THINGS. It is full to the brim with original ways to furnish and decorate. The homes have been grouped by theme or style, to make it easier to appreciate the concepts behind each one and to see where you instinctively feel a connection. There will be spaces that might alarm but others that will surprise and delight and form the seed of an idea that you can adapt to suit you and your life. What that turns out to be is entirely up to you.

← In George and Diana Shaw's home, a gray-and-white abstract painting provides the perfect backdrop to this decorative flower display, bought from an antique store in Long Island and sprayed white, in keeping with the monochrome palette of this bedroom.

In the foreground of Tim Hartley's bedroom, sat on a small white table, is a large Diptyque candle. The small Saarinen table displays a selection of carefully selected items, in shades of gray, black, and silver. The tall black floor lamp is by Flos.

Modernism refers to a period in history when there was a real aesthetic shift in art and architecture. At the time, it was considered avant-garde, but now it doesn't feel at all unorthodox. In the mid-20th century, there was a real explosion of innovative design in furniture, brought about, in particular, by the arrival of designers from Scandinavia who helped to shape our lives. The homes on the following pages are examples of how successfully modern, cutting-edge design can be worked into period houses, creating original and comfortable living spaces.

ART-LOVING MODERNISTS

1

FAMILY FASHION

Patric and Christina Shaw live in an early 20th-century Brooklyn brownstone with their two sons, Callum and Alex, both students, and Georgie, the dog. Patric, who was born in England, is a fashion photographer and met Christina, who worked in the fashion industry, in her native Australia. The move to New York came about primarily for Patric's business. After a stint living in Manhattan, THEY CHOSE TO SETTLE IN FORT GREENE, A LEAFY NEIGHBORHOOD OF BROOKLYN, WITH A WONDERFUL CREATIVE VIBE, FULL OF LIKE-MINDED PEOPLE.

PATRIC AND CHRISTINA TOOK SEVERAL YEARS RENOVATING THE FOUR-STORY HOUSE FROM TOP TO BOTTOM, BUT IT WAS CERTAINLY WORTH THE WAIT. It is now absolutely stunning. Each and every feature was treated with the utmost care and attention, sensitively repaired and restored where necessary. Architecturally beautiful, the house contains all of its original features, including magnificent marble fireplaces, ornate staircases, and paneled doors. Large imposing windows fill the house with light, and the spacious rooms with their high ceilings make it the perfect living environment for a family. The couple's discerning eye and desire for perfection mean that every single detail is exactly as it should be.

IN SPITE OF ALL THIS HISTORY, THE HOME HAS A VERY MODERN FEEL, WHICH IS DOWN TO HOW THE COUPLE HAVE FILLED IT. Their passion for culture and the arts is evident in the books and paintings on display, which include some of Patric's fashion photography, and their love of contemporary furniture and furnishings is displayed in every room. White paintwork through the entire house makes the perfect neutral backdrop for the various pieces.

⬆ These paneled double doors with the graceful arch above are just one of the many original features of this period house. The staircase wall has been taken back to the brickwork, then lightly painted white, adding to the sense of history.

◄ Informal collections of artwork feature throughout the house. On top of the **1960s** sliding door sideboard in **Patric's** office space is an eclectic display, including a painting by **Patric**, and a **Guy Bourdin** photograph of a **Zandra Rhodes** creation, taken for British Vogue.

In the master bedroom, the mantelpiece is decorated informally with art and photographs. A long glass-top table gives extra height to the green retro glass table lamp and supports the "Happy Box," filled with family treasures.

Georgie enjoys the Eames leather lounge chair as much as everyone else. In direct contrast with such iconic design is the beautifully textured piece of driftwood leaning against the wall.

Like the other rooms, this living space has been decorated in subtle tones, but with the clever use of stronger colors in the yellow retro lamp and the lime-green cushion on the wool sofa. Once again, the juxtaposition of unlikely partners —the marble fireplace and the Saarinen Tulip table—is a success.

The house provides a gorgeous historic backdrop to an exciting mix of contemporary furniture and furnishings. RESTORED WITH GREAT SENSITIVITY AND DECORATED WITH EQUAL CARE AND CONSIDERATION, IT IS A SUBTLE MIX OF STYLES BUT WITH A LEAN TOWARD THE MID-20TH CENTURY. Iconic pieces have been put together with great skill by Patric and Christina, ensuring that the end result is a home that's comfortable and easy to live in. The house is on four floors altogether. These pictures show the third-floor master bedroom and living room, where the whole family (and dog) go to relax. WHITE WALLS AND PAINTWORK HAVE ALLOWED THE COUPLE TO BE MORE ADVENTUROUS WITH THEIR FURNITURE AND FURNISHINGS. The retro lamp by the window, with its acid-yellow base, was an enviable find at a vintage market—a real gem. A worn animal skin partly covers the original floorboards, while LIGHT IS SOFTLY FILTERED THROUGH LINEN CURTAINS. PIECES OF ART ARE EVIDENT ALL THROUGH THE HOUSE, MOSTLY CREATED BY MEMBERS OF THE FAMILY, WHO ARE ALL CREATIVE AND SKILLED ARTISTS.

Art is evident in every room, testament to the creative skills of all the family

◄◄◄ In the office studio, the narrow floorboards, which run throughout the house, have been sanded, stained, and restored to their original splendor. Yet another beautiful marble fireplace is central to this space. The creativity at work is evident in the piles of magazines, paints, laptops, and the easel.

▲ As you turn into the main living room immediately after
▲ entering the house, you are greeted by this spectacular piece of art by Patric and Christina's eldest son, Alexander, which manages to dwarf yet another ornate marble fireplace. A Berber rug adds a softness to the floorboards and brings comfort to the space.

►►► At one end of the mantelpiece is a mix of carefully curated vases and pots, which have been collected over time. Put together with skill and care, they are a unique addition to this living space.

The fitted shelving system, out of sight as you enter the living room, is home to the many books collected over the years by the family. One unit is used to house a collection of shared treasures, carefully arranged to give a pleasing display of mostly white objects.

➤ A carved African mask makes a bold statement on the mantelpiece, its color tone a perfect partner to the aged marble and the dark wood mirror. Dried grasses bring a subtle softness to the display, while a family photograph tucked into the mirror adds a personal touch.

Their discerning eye and desire for perfection mean that every single detail is exactly as it should be

Moving through the upstairs living room, you enter the kitchen, an open, modern, and well-organized space. The windows to the back look out onto the yard below. A long cabinet fits against the wall, its open shelves housing neatly stacked piles of the family's everyday china. Hidden behind the sliding doors are less attractive kitchen essentials. THE LARGE PIECES OF ART ARE BY PATRIC AND SON ALEXANDER. THEY MAKE UP WHAT APPEARS TO BE A CASUAL DISPLAY BUT, together with the carved mask protected under a glass dome and the unusual candlesticks, IT IS, IN FACT, METICULOUSLY THOUGHT-OUT AND ORGANIZED. A long wooden dining table, complemented by white Saarinen chairs, is perfect for family meals as well as entertaining. A single lily in a vase is all that's needed to dress the space.

White walls and paintwork work
well with the soft tones of the
wooden dining table and the trim
on the cabinets. Patric's "New York"
painting is propped up against the
chimney breast next to "Coki,"
another painting by son Alexander.
White, industrial-style uplights are
evenly spaced on either side.

This spacious room at the very top of the house is designed upside down, with narrow floorboards used for the ceiling, and the floor painted white. It makes a great den for the boys to hang out with their friends or simply chill and watch movies.

ART AT ITS HEART

←◼ An eclectic mix of pictures decorates one of the dining room walls. There is nothing calculated or precious about the display—it is simply one that gives pleasure to its owners. The surreal oil on canvas by Djordje Ozbolt shows Hercules taming a hyena. Alongside, the running man is by Dame Elisabeth Frink. She is a favorite artist of both Betty and David. Another larger piece by her can be seen in the hall. ◼—➤

This amazing house in west London is the home of Betty Jackson, one of the best-known names in British fashion, and her husband and business partner David Cohen. Betty and I met many years ago when I was working as a fashion buyer. I fell in love with her designs and bought them. We've remained in touch ever since.

THE COUPLE HAVE LIVED IN THIS DOUBLE-FRONTED PERIOD HOUSE FOR MANY YEARS, INITIALLY WITH THEIR TWO CHILDREN who have now flown the nest and are forging their own careers: Oliver is an actor, while Pascale works in PR for New York jewelry designer Alexis Bittar. AS SOON AS YOU WALK THROUGH THE FRONT DOOR, YOU KNOW THAT THERE ARE TALENTED, ARTISTIC MINDS AT WORK INSIDE. A glass extension built onto the dining room at the back floods the downstairs with natural light. Everyone entering the house for the first time is in awe at how fabulous it is.

ALTHOUGH THE PREVAILING LOOK IS MODERNIST, BETTY AND DAVID HAVE CLEVERLY WOVEN IN OTHER ELEMENTS, MIXING DIFFERENT STYLES, to create a stunning home that is unpretentious and a place where everyone feels immediately welcome. There is original art hanging on more or less every wall. IT IS AN ECLECTIC COLLECTION THAT HAS BEEN GATHERED OVER TIME, FROM PAINTINGS BY UP-AND-COMING AND ESTABLISHED ARTISTS TO ILLUSTRATIONS MADE BY THEIR CHILDREN WHEN YOUNG. Some of the artists are known to the couple personally, which makes the collection even more significant. Each piece calls out to be studied up close and appreciated.

David's favorite room for relaxation is at the front of the house. Modernist yet comfortable, it is furnished with wide, '60s-style armchairs and cushions in retro-style fabrics. These, together with the floor lamp, with its black pleated shade and legs like a tripod, and the glass-topped side table, create a comfortable nook for reading and watching TV. David and Betty's keen eye for contemporary British art is evident in the oil on canvas by Philip Davies.

Betty and David are expert at
making their space work for them.
They knocked down most of a
dividing wall to create a lovely long
through room. By leaving the central
chimney breast, where they have
installed a modern, open, gas fire,
they have prevented the room from
looking like a corridor. The chimney
breast is the perfect place to display
a Brian Bolger charcoal drawing.
Bolger used to design fabric prints
for Betty's collections during the
'80s. Above the bronze sculpture,
another piece by Dame Elisabeth
Frink, is a Glen Baxter painting of
men in raincoats, highlighting yet
again the diversity in the couple's
art collection.

Knowing how to mix colors, textures, and styles comes as second nature to Betty. NEUTRAL-COLORED PAINTWORK THROUGHOUT MAKES THE IDEAL BACKDROP FOR THE ESOTERIC COLLECTION OF ART. It also showcases the various pieces of furniture, whether design classics or not, to perfection. In Betty's favorite sitting room, shown on the left, Arne Jacobsen chairs look completely at ease with a cowhide rug and a low-slung coffee table made from a solid lump of wood.

◄◄ᴄ This sitting room is where Betty likes to relax. Kingfisher-blue Swan chairs by **Arne Jacobsen** and a white leather, button-back Chesterfield sofa make their distinctive design statements but without competing with each other. Surrounded by white, the large oil on canvas by **David Band** above the sofa, originally the design for a Spandau Ballet album cover, draws the eye even more. The spherical, metal pendant lamp is by **Moooi**.

◄◄ᴄ Neatly curated, a double-decker row of black-and-white framed photographs of the family makes a welcoming display in the hall. The contrasting painting on the mantelpiece in the background is shown in close-up on the next page.

▲ This sitting room is another example of laid-back design, where designer furniture provides both style and comfort. The glossy orange and white **Natasha Law** painting makes a striking companion for the gray linen **Philippe Starck** sofa.

Everything on display in this home is there because it is loved. As you would expect, there is no design conformity: FINE ART SITS ALONGSIDE PICTURES DRAWN BY THE CHILDREN; modern glass tea-light holders adorn an ornate period marble fireplace. THE DISPLAYS, FREQUENTLY WITH UNEXPECTED PAIRINGS, INTRIGUE AND DELIGHT. ABOVE THE FIREPLACE IN DAVID'S FAVORED SITTING ROOM IS A CONTEMPORARY OIL ON CANVAS BY EDWARD KAY. Inspired by art history and kitsch, Kay's take on 18th-century portraiture accompanies the little framed picture by Jane Fox Hipple. Vases and pitchers of fresh flowers are dotted around the house but their presence is never intrusive. A stone pot of paperwhite narcissi is a simple addition to the uncrowded mantelpiece.

↑ A contemporary Edward Kay oil on canvas, resembling an old master, makes an unlikely but successful companion for the small framed picture drawn by American artist Jane Fox Hipple. Bookending the display are a retro-style glass ornament and a tall, sinuous metal candlestick.

↑ White and green are the theme of this apparently effortless shelf display. Porcelain pitchers, a jolly Buddha, and a glass table lamp share the space with glass vases and a striking portrait of a girl with a brooding green background. This was painted by their daughter **Pascale**.

Betty and David have always loved to travel, and still do. PART OF THE PLEASURE COMES FROM SHOPPING IN MARKETS NEAR AND FAR, AND RETURNING HOME WITH VARIOUS TREASURES AND TRINKETS. WITH AN UNERRING INSTINCT FOR CREATING COLLECTIONS, THEY ARE EXPERTS AT GATHERING INDIVIDUAL PIECES FROM ALL OVER, knowing what they will work with and where when they get back home. The lustrous porcelain pitchers shown above look as if they are part of a set, but these were all bought on separate occasions, although with the express intention of displaying them together. The smiling Buddha alongside, another one-off purchase, looks as if he has always belonged with them.

The master bathroom is a purely functional room but one that does not lose out on design. Muted gray, skimmed concrete walls form the backdrop to a long, white trough basin. The chrome fittings are modern and streamlined, adding to the quietly efficient ambience.

THE MASTER BEDROOM IS ALSO STRIPPED BACK TO THE BARE ESSENTIALS SO THAT NOTHING CAN INTRUDE ON A GOOD NIGHT'S SLEEP. AN ENTIRE WALL OF GLASS BATHES THE ROOM IN NATURAL LIGHT, TO BE SHUT OUT BY A WHITE ROLLER BLIND AT THE FLICK OF A REMOTE-CONTROL SWITCH. The neutral color scheme soothes and relaxes. Clothes and shoes are hidden away in floor-to-ceiling cupboards either side of the dressing room, enforcing the sense of tranquility.

⬆ Flush with the walls, floor-to-ceiling cupboards run either side of the dressing room, offering masses of storage space for clothes and shoes.

Just a step away from the bedroom is the master bathroom, a streamlined and pared-back haven of peace and quiet. Gray, skimmed concrete walls form a soothing backdrop for the contemporary chrome fittings and white, ceramic trough sink

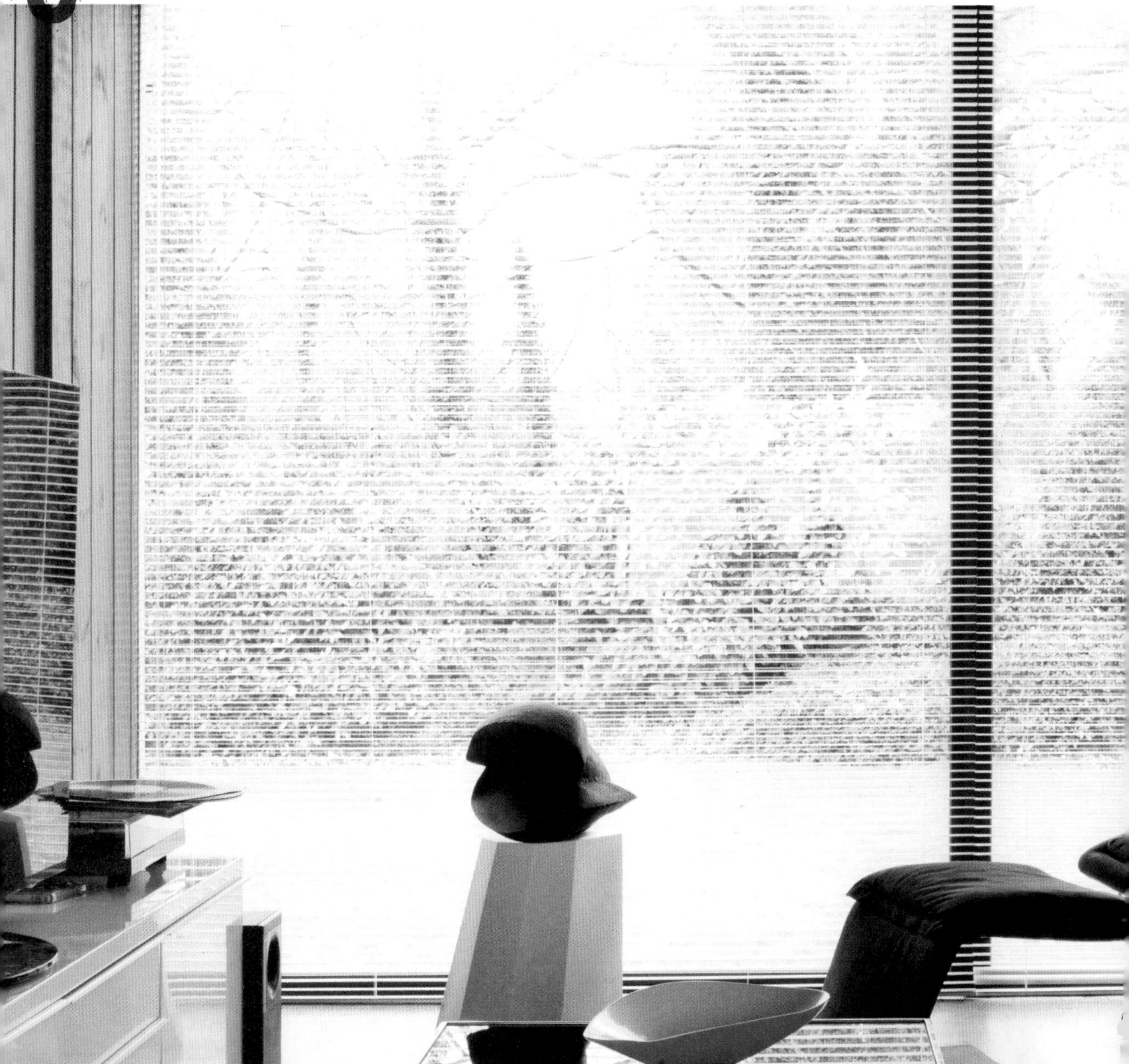

CREATIVE HEAD SPACE

This unique house, on the outskirts of a charming village in the Berkshire countryside, could have been built with Tim Hartley, its present owner, in mind. TIM HAS LIVED HERE FOR FIVE YEARS AND FURNISHED IT EXPERTLY, ALL THE WHILE KEEPING IN MIND THE BUILDING'S HERITAGE. DESIGNED IN THE EARLY 1960S BY THE INFLUENTIAL ARCHITECT PETER FOGGO, this "Space House" is a one-story, light-filled structure of cedarwood, steel, and glass cubes. Of huge architectural merit, it is one of three houses in the same style set back behind beech hedges. Tim knew this was the house for him, so he knocked at the door and asked the owners if they would be interested in selling. They were, and a few months later Tim moved in.

Formerly creative director at Vidal Sassoon and now a freelance art director who oversees hairdressing shows and photoshoots all over the world, TIM HAS A GREAT LOVE OF 20TH-CENTURY STYLE AND DESIGN, PARTICULARLY FROM THE 1960S. His impeccable taste has led to some amazing purchases from that era, and this modern and very functional home is the perfect showcase for them. The house is spacious, with generous proportions. Every room, including the five bedrooms, is filled with art and furniture that Tim has carefully collected to suit his home, all with a unique tale to tell.

◄◄ As well as blocking out the sun, the narrow, brushed-steel **Venetian** blinds give a graphic edge to the enormous window, which extends across the height and breadth of the sitting room. The ultrasuede **Saporitalia** reclining chair and footstool, along with the **Saarinen** occasional tables that once graced **Pan Am's** glamorous offices in New York, suit this pared-down space perfectly.

◄◄ The original cedarwood floors run through most of the house, providing a feeling of warmth. A number of the rooms also have cedarwood-paneled walls, making painting and decorating unnecessary.

↑ The Icelandic goatskin throw ↑ softens the look as well as the feel of this setting at the marble-topped dining table.

⇒⇒ White, molded plastic Charles and Ray Eames chairs, reissued from the 1950s, and a white Cappellini wooden cabinet with a high-gloss finish stand cheek by jowl with a gold-colored pig by Pols Potten, adding a touch of glitter and humor. A Martinelli Cobra desk lamp throws light onto the art above.

Tim's choice of furniture and decoration, from molded plastic chairs to shaggy goatskin throws, gives a real sense of the period of the building. HIS LOVE FOR THE '60S IS DEEP-ROOTED AND INSTINCTIVE, MAKING IT EASY FOR HIM TO FURNISH HIS HOME IN THIS WAY. Although the overall look is undeniably straight-edged and male, his love of beautiful things means that it avoids being soulless and cold.

Around the marble-topped dining table, Charles and Ray Eames chairs—aluminum and leather as well as molded plastic—are further examples of 20th-century design classics. Softening the space are a cowhide rug and a neutral-colored Scandinavian woolen rug in the adjoining seating area. Above the leather Cappellini sofa hangs an Andy Warhol print, the reflected strips of another set of Venetian blinds scoring the face of this 1960s icon.

◄◄ An office space need never be dreary. In this part of the living area, overseen by a Modesty Blaise print, a white Cobra lamp casts light over the Walter Albini glass desk. A green, cloth-covered Eames chair completes the picture.

▼ Tim keeps all his art and fashion books collected over the years on chunky wooden shelves. The one-legged Bonzanini table in the room beyond was a gift from Vidal Sassoon, a dear friend.

▷► Art is the main feature of this room, with three pieces of the "Brute" by Robert Loughlin on top of the beautiful, flat-fronted sideboard. A plastic fly, larger than life, is an intriguing and humorous partner to the sputnik table lamp.

Much of the house is open-plan, with reception and seating areas leading seamlessly into each other. Where there are doors, separating bedrooms, for example, these are white and flat-fronted, in the original '60s style. Similarly, where the walls are not made of cedarwood, they are painted a gloss white.

Tim is a keen collector of mid-20th-century art, and each piece is highlighted to best effect with the ambient lighting-there are no pendants to intrude upon the warm interior. His choice of lighting, from a sputnik table light and floor-standing ball lamp to simple Danish metal candlesticks, reflects his love of modern design.

As well as hanging pictures from the walls, Tim uses the tops of pieces of furniture to display his original artwork. Three of Robert Loughlin's signature paintings of his square-jawed "Brute" are propped up casually against the wall, belying their worth.

Unlike the living areas, the bedrooms and bathrooms are painted white with white floorboards to give a sense of privacy and detachment from the rest of the house

◄◄ A framed poster featuring a headless David by Michelangelo is central to this idiosyncratic display in the master bedroom. Sharing the space on top of the mid-20th-century Meredew chest of drawers is a collection of vintage cologne bottles and blue glass. Even though the diagonal strip above is part of the supporting steel framework of the house, it has been cleverly worked into the display.

The displays on these black floating shelves in the guest bedroom show the same attention to detail found elsewhere. Although the look is hard-edged, pared-down, and masculine, the passion of its owner still shines through.

Soothing, comfortable, and almost monochrome, the master bedroom, with floor-to-ceiling doors opening out onto the garden, is Tim's favorite part of the house. It also contains one of his favorite pieces: the **1950s** French articulated lamp by the bed on the white Saarinen table. The metal-framed glass table on wheels is a **1955** Bauhaus design, its clean lines kept free of extraneous clutter. Tim had the gorgeous cushion covers made from '60s headscarves.

There is more than a passing resemblance between the master and guest bathrooms, and, unlike the rest of the house, these rooms have been recently refurbished by Tim to bring them completely up to date. THEY ARE MODERN, SLEEK SPACES AND COMPLETELY FUNCTIONAL, WITH STATE-OF-THE-ART ENAMEL FIXTURES AND CHROME FITTINGS. NEVERTHELESS, TIM HASN'T NEGLECTED TO INJECT THEM WITH PERSONALITY IN THE FORM OF DISPLAYS OF COLORED RETRO GLASS BOTTLES ON SIMPLE GLASS SHELVES. A soya candle with a cotton wick by Cire Trudon, portraying a classical bust, makes a lovely decorative bookend to the glass collection in the master bathroom. In spite of its sound ecological credentials, the candle will probably never be burned, simply because it would ruin the display.

Both spaces are primarily white, with large, rectangular white tiles covering the walls, floors, and bath surrounds, giving a unified look. In the master bathroom, a light well clad in dark wood directs additional light onto the shelf display.

Simple decorative displays of retro glass bottles in different colors give personality to otherwise purely functional spaces

◄◄ Light streams down through the light well clad in dark wood into the master bathroom, spotlighting the display of colored retro glass bottles and the candle in the shape of a classical bust.

↑ A similar display of colored retro glass bottles is a fitting decorative addition to the guest bathroom, contrasting beautifully with the sleek chrome taps and streamlined enamel bathtub.

➤➤ In the master bathroom, the molded plastic caddy with swing-out trays for holding bathroom toiletries is a design classic on casters by Joe Colombo from the **1970s**, originally used by architects as an office organizer. Above, the **1960s** Chrome Pistillo sputnik light fitting sends out shafts of light.

2 LIVING WITH PATTERN & COLOR

It is hard to believe that my apartment features in this chapter because I've always been known for having white in my home. Color has come to me late in my decorating style, and that's why I say that if you like the idea of color and feel inspired by it, take a chance and try it out. A word of warning, though: don't get caught in the trap of trying to match everything—that's when it will all feel contrived. Mix up the patterns and colors, like all the homes featured in this chapter. Start off gradually and see where it takes you. You never know, you may start to love color as much as I do.

◄█ █►► The painting of a ballet dress by Laurence Amélie hangs in my living room above the cream sofa. Its striking colors are reflected in the antique decorative mirror, surrounded by various green glass jars and vases and Laurence's old paint pots.

EVERCHANGING DISPLAY

It's fair to say that I move something in my home almost every day and, since my daughter moved out, I do it even more because I now have a spare room with which to experiment. I guess this all stems from working in the world of homeware and gifts—I am constantly tempted by new things and can't resist adding them to my home. FORTUNATELY, I HAVE BECOME QUITE GOOD AT EDITING, BUT I AM NOT WHAT YOU WOULD CALL A MINIMALIST.

←⊂ Another old mirror, with foxing adding to its charm, is propped up on the painted chest of drawers. The art and vintage finds share a common finish of white and aged patina, uniting the display. A limited edition print of Tracey Emin's "Walking Around My World" hangs over the mirror. Equally precious are the photograph and drawing by Richard Nott and a porcelain tureen decorated with hand-molded roses on the lid.

↑ Leaning against the white wall, on top of a long, dark gray console table, is an old mirror. This forms the backdrop to an informal display of a white hydrangea in a beautifully aged plant pot, a glass vase of contorted twigs, and a French crystal-drop light.

⊃→ The glass-fronted cabinet is both handsome and functional, housing all my glassware and china. Adding a note of glamour to the table, which is set for a simple afternoon tea, is an antique French crystal chandelier.

Wherever I use bold colors, I am likely to have white or toned-down color accessories. FOR AS LONG AS I CAN REMEMBER, I HAVE HAD TWO PALE CREAM SOFAS, WHICH I SIMPLY UPDATE BY ADDING DIFFERENT COLORED THROWS. I recently painted the floors throughout a dark gray, and I'm really pleased with the result–it somehow pulls the apartment together. I also dyed the dining tablecloth to match and changed all the wall art to white. My home has suddenly taken on a completely new look.

I get up early every day of the week for work, so relaxing at weekends is very important to me. DRINKING A CUP OF TEA AND READING THE NEWSPAPERS IN MY EVER SO COMFORTABLE BED, WITH BEAUTIFULLY SOFT, WHITE LINEN SHEETS AND PLENTY OF PILLOWS, IS HEAVEN.

Weekend evenings are usually spent relaxing and entertaining—my kitchen is the perfect size for casual suppers with friends. Eddie, the rescue Jack Russell, joined the household this year. My daughter and I share him, but he lives with me for most of the time. He has definitely made home feel more like home, and he also makes everyone else welcome!

A big comfy bed, top-quality bed linen, and plenty of pillows are for me a necessity, not an indulgence. Similarly, a cup of tea never tastes better than when served in a porcelain cup—here, a Coalport white cabbage design.

COMFORT AND COLOR

Kyle Andrew lives with her husband Rick and their two children, Baz and Rei, in Brooklyn, New York. Their federal-style house, built in the mid-1800s, has had many additions made to it over the course of time. The couple have taken five years to create the colorful, comfortable, and sunny home it is today. THE RENOVATION WAS THOUGHTFUL AND TRUE TO THE PERIOD AND STYLE OF THE HOUSE, WHEREAS THE DECORATIONS ARE BOLD, INCORPORATING RICH TEXTURES AND TEXTILES WITH ETHNIC TOUCHES THROUGHOUT. The large spacious rooms flow easily from one to the other.

Kyle travels to the city each day for her job as brand director for Kate Spade Saturday, the new line from Kate Spade New York, which is famous for its use of color. Kyle, too, embraces color wholeheartedly in her home, from wallpaper and tablecloths to bed covers and cushions. I am also a fan of color and I really appreciate the skill with which she and Rick have incorporated it into their lives.

◄◄ A chaise longue, covered with an orange, floral-patterned Florence Broadhurst print, sits by the master bedroom window, overlooking the front yard. For me, it is a real luxury to have enough space in a bedroom simply to relax, and the well-proportioned rooms in this house allow just that. This corner, with the carved wooden fireplace and the vase of magnolia leaves on top, resembles a sitting room.

↑ An oval folding table in the bedroom is used purely for display. In this small vignette, books act as a plinth to give extra height and provide balance. The framed picture above is by Kyle's sister, Lisa Andrew. A small wall sconce is a decorative as well as practical feature.

➤➤ Hunting for treasures is one of Kyle's favorite pastimes. This collection of Madonnas and other religious figurines makes an impressive group on a shelf in the living room. A long, curled horn leads the eye to a pair of old paintings.

With windows on the side and the
front of the living room, this space
is filled with light. What I find most
striking about its decoration is the
collection of Indian art and mirrors
gathered together on one wall. It
works so well because their shapes
and finish are all complementary.
Enforcing the ethnic feel, as well
as adding color and texture, are
the kilim cushions and a throw
from Uzbekistan.

←◄ The entrance hall appears quite traditional in style, with dark wood paneling reaching halfway up the wall, topped by a set of framed vintage prints of birds. However, a surprise blast of color is introduced by the unusually long bench covered in richly colored stripes. Originally used by customers at a Kate Spade store for trying on shoes, it looks very much at home here.

⊃→ A bold and sunny Florence Broadhurst print wallpaper meets you at the top of the dark wooden staircase leading to the first floor.

When entering this home, which I did early on a sunny winter's morning, the atmosphere was warm and easy. I felt so welcome and could imagine myself living here. COLOR GREETS YOU AS SOON AS YOU ENTER THE LONG HALLWAY. The bench, upholstered in a multicolored striped fabric, makes A TYPICALLY BOLD AND, AT THE SAME TIME, WELCOMING STATEMENT.

Two doors lead off the hallway into the living room (see pages 60–1), where tall sash windows look out onto the front yard. Comfortable squashy sofas are adorned with cushions covered in kilims and a throw from Uzbekistan. The exotic theme is continued with the display on the main wall, where pictures from India of religious icons and gods rub shoulders with small decorative mirrors.

The decoration is bold, incorporating rich textures and textiles

◄── Bentwood dining chairs encircle the family table in the dining room. The very bold red and blue cloth is nothing more than I would expect from this colorful home.

▶─▶ The white paneled walls highlight the dark bentwood chairs and console table. The piece of ethnic cloth acting as a runner on top of the table and the **1960s** zebra skin rug introduce alternative cultural references. Just a sliver of the painting by Kyle's sister Lisa can be seen above the console table.

Color, with ethnic references, is the order of the day in this modern home

Back through the hall and into the dining room, there are more ethnic touches, with an old zebra skin rug from the 1960s under the slatted wood coffee table, and a brightly colored cloth runner on top of the console table.

Climbing the dark wood staircase to the next floor, one's eyes can't help but be fixed on the vibrant, orange bird-motif wallpaper (see page 63). This is one of twelve prints that Kate Spade has bought from the archive of the 20th-century Australian designer Florence Broadhurst and which she uses for textiles and wallpapers. In the master bedroom (see pages 66–7), a Florence Broadhurst print covers a chaise longue and also the cushions on the bed. The bedroom is vast, and Kyle has created clever and comfortable niches in which to relax and enjoy the sunshine as it bathes the room in light.

KYLE HAS A MAGPIE INSTINCT. WEEKENDS ARE SPENT FORAGING AT FLEA MARKETS AND ANTIQUES FAIRS, WHILE EXOTIC VACATIONS ABROAD ALWAYS INVOLVE VISITS TO BAZAARS AND FÊTES, hence the many multicultural references in the home. Kyle's collections are organized by theme, including statues of religious icons, pieces of pewter, decorative mirrors, and Indian art. Kyle's sister Lisa, who lives in Australia, is the artist in the family, and there are at least ten pictures in Kyle and Rick's home that she has painted. They make big, bold statements, totally in keeping with the rest of the decoration.

In the master bedroom, a piece of ethereal art of Coney Island by Lisa Andrew, Kyle's sister, forms the backdrop to an enormous fern and a weathered and beaten-up old chair. Much too dilapidated to sit on, the chair adds character to the room. A wall of sheer voile curtains hides the windows and highlights the bed and the selection of cushions in Florence Broadhurst prints. The largest one matches the sofa on the other side of the room (see page 58).

CASUAL LAID-BACK ELEGANCE

I first met Ornella Pisano in around 2002. It was at a trade show in New York City, where I WAS LITERALLY STOPPED IN MY TRACKS BY HER BEAUTIFUL FURNITURE AND ACCESSORIES. I HAD NEVER SEEN SUCH ORIGINAL AND EXQUISITELY CRAFTED HOME DECORATION. It was spellbinding and I just had to talk to her and discover everything about her work.

Ornella came to New York from her native Venice during the mid-1980s, and quickly joined the art scene. HER PREVIOUS EXPOSURE TO THE BEAUTY OF BYZANTINE CHURCHES AND ALL THE CULTURAL REFERENCES FROM HER HOME INFLUENCED HER DESIGNS AND WHAT SHE WANTED TO DO. SHE LITERALLY SAW THE WORLD THROUGH MOSAIC LENSES, and so began Ercole Home, creating pieces of mosaic furniture and decor that are also works of art. She very quickly built a reputation among interior designers and design stores around the world, desperate to buy into her unique style.

↑ A small square vintage table with turned legs houses a charming and eclectic display, indicative of Ornella's unique decorating style.

←◄ The warm yellow walls are a non-intrusive backdrop for the various pieces of art, including those displayed on the carved mantelpiece.

←◄ ←◄ Framed by the tall sash window in the dining room, overlooking the backyard, this is the perfect space to rest after one of Ornella's wonderful Italian lunches. A velvet slipper chair and a large, fringe-trimmed cushion provide the creature comforts.

Hanging on the dining room wall is a picture of the house, a very good likeness, painted by the gardener. The vivid blue sky mirrors the color of the sofa, which pops color into the room and makes a distinct contrast against the pale mottled walls. Both the ornate Venetian chandelier and the wall sconce are from Ercole.

This big, old farmhouse is the rural retreat in Columbia County, upstate New York, for Ornella, husband Pietro, a musician, and Arthur the dog, when life in the city gets too much. Their three children are all grown up now and have left home, but they still like to join their parents at weekends in this family home. WHAT I LOVE ABOUT ORNELLA'S STYLE IS THAT IT IS LITERALLY HER OWN. I REALLY WOULD STRUGGLE TO SAY IT RESEMBLES THIS OR THAT, or that it reminds me of various other things. It simply doesn't. I love the way she mixes up so many different colors, styles, and fabrics. The combined effect is very comfortable, very understated.

↑ Bold, black-and-white patterned
↑ wallpaper and two mosaic mirrors
line the walls of the hallway leading
to the dining room, where the
inviting table is set for lunch.

▶▶ , ▶▶ ▶▶ Ornella's clever
way of combining different patterns
is apparent with this table setting.
The tablecloth, with a white
background and rust-colored flowers,
is partially covered by a runner in
the same color tones but a different
pattern. Meanwhile, the linen napkins,
again with the same color tones but
striped, are made from heavy linen.
The cream plates, with their
scalloped edges, and the lovely,
antique-looking silverware with
bone handles, are a lovely contrast
with the turquoise bowls. The old
dining chairs have gently curved
backs, adding to the overall effect
of casual elegance.

THIS HOUSE WAS INCREDIBLY EASY TO PHOTOGRAPH, AS THERE ARE LOTS OF SETTINGS WITHIN IT THAT ARE SO APPEALING AND, **LIKE MANY OF THE OTHER HOMES FEATURED IN THIS BOOK, IT HAS ITS OWN UNIQUE REFERENCES.** Built over three levels more than a hundred years ago, the house has a number of quirky nooks and crannies, where the children must have acted out many adventures when they were young.

A small vintage pedestal table, with a wonderfully worn patina, houses an idiosyncratic selection of decorative finds, including a small, colorful ornament of two birds and candlestick saucers with china lilies protruding from them. The very spindly chair, with a piece of decorative floral fabric thrown over its back, and the two vintage oil paintings are the finishing touches to this vignette that resembles a still-life painting.

The bold patterned wallpaper that lines the downstairs hallway is continued up to the first floor landing. Here, too, the original wide floorboards have been sanded but left bare. Lighting the narrow space is a small Ercole glass chandelier with colorful glass fruit hanging from it.

Looking out from one of the bedrooms to the landing, one sees the striking combination of the black-and-white wallpaper and the rich rust-colored velvet chair, with its beige and white patterned cushion.

▣▶ Guests arriving at the house in winter are greeted by a blazing wood fire and an overwhelming sense of history, as revealed in the low, original beams and exposed brickwork. This room is an exceptionally cozy place to drink tea after a day working outside. Shelves have been incorporated into the soaring chimney breast. A vintage doll's house sits on the upper ledge, along with a selection of smaller vintage houses. Adding to the sense of history is a long candleholder hanging from the high ceiling by a chain.

▣▶ ▣▶ Opposite the fireplace, a table holds all the information for local community events, such as farmers' markets, fairs, and so on. Although a practical space, it still bears Ornella's decorative touch, including a bold print of a peacock, an ornate gold photo frame, a beaten metal table lamp with a tasseled shade, and, rather strangely, a papier-mâché snowman.

Ornella, Pietro, and Arthur the dog spend many weekends at their country retreat, especially as the journey takes less than three hours from their apartment in New York City. THERE IS A HUGE AMOUNT OF LAND AROUND THE HOUSE, WHICH IS JUST THE RIGHT ANTIDOTE FOR STIFLING CITY LIFE. THE COUPLE HAVE IMMERSED THEMSELVES IN THE LOCAL COMMUNITY AND MADE A LOT OF FRIENDS IN THE AREA. Many impromptu gatherings take place around the fireplace in the winter months, accompanied by big bowls of homemade soup and Pietro playing his guitar. It's just what you would expect from Italian hospitality.

The farmhouse is very spacious, and there are plenty
of guest rooms for the children and the many friends that
frequently come to visit. THE HOUSE IS A GOOD, EASY
LIVING SHAPE IN WHICH THE WELL-PROPORTIONED ROOMS SIT
COMFORTABLY. GENEROUS-SIZE SASH WINDOWS IN EVERY ROOM FILL IT
WITH LIGHT FROM ALL ANGLES as the sun travels across the sky.
THERE ARE MIXTURES OF COLORS AND TEXTURES THROUGHOUT,
with the walls a combination of brightly colored paint
and dramatic wallpaper prints. Vintage ceramics and art
collected over the years fill the space, but there are also
many pieces of Ercole mosaic furniture. This has a way of
looking vintage itself, and each piece becomes an heirloom
for the future.

↑ The cabinet next to the bed is an
Ercole mosaic washstand. Broken
pieces of vintage china, in a curlicue
pattern dotted with butterflies, make
up its top. The cupboard doors
are painted green, and vintage
wallpaper has been laid in the door
panels. The delicate metal framework
of the bed and the vintage
candleholder are romantic extras.

➤ A small square table with a
tiled top holds yet another decorative
lamp. The quality bed linen, in soft
tones with an embroidered trim, is
perfect for a guest room.

←⚏ Many of the windows in the house are left undressed but wherever privacy is needed, there are sheer, white cotton shades. Decorative vintage candleholders make gorgeous bedside lights. This ornate example, made from Italian glass, is set off to perfection against the blind.

⚓ The vintage oil painting on canvas in this guest bedroom depicts fairies in a garden. Its whimsical subject matter strikes a chord with the small decorative console shelf beneath and the vintage ceramic deer and cart.

As you look at these pictures of Ornella and Pietro's rural retreat, I hope that, like me, you come away feeling inspired. By that I don't mean that you should aim to replicate Ornella's style but rather **EMULATE HER CASUAL, LAID-BACK APPROACH TO LIVING,** WHICH IS SO VERY APPARENT IN THE WAY SHE HAS PUT TOGETHER THIS DREAM OF A COUNTRY HOME. The look she has created is altogether individual, which in itself speaks volumes about her.

The original covered outbuilding houses logs for the fire, gardening tools, and a table and chairs for informal indoor dining. The top of the Ercole table is inlaid with mosaic tiles. Its spindly metal legs complement those of the chairs. The open door leads through to the house.

The entire house bears Ornella's stamp of casual, laid-back elegance

⬆ The painted metal wall sconce from Ercole has been made to look vintage. So very pretty, it holds two candles that will add a romantic glow to the space as the light fades. Sitting on the brick ledge above is a framed drawing of a coat of arms. Who but Ornella would think to put these two distinctive and unconnected pieces together, creating such a beautiful yet simple display?

ANTHROPOLOGICAL FINDS

Gisela Garcia Escuela moved to London in 1993 from her native Spain. Seven years later, she met her Italian husband Francesco Monge while walking on London's Primrose Hill. Together, they bought this loft space in Borough, on the south side of the River Thames. The building was originally a school dating from 1910, and their apartment is in the section where boys were once taught. THE AREA HAS BEEN TRANSFORMED IN RECENT YEARS INTO A BUZZING, CREATIVE HUB, WITH COOL BARS AND RESTAURANTS, AND THE BEST FARMERS' MARKETS THAT THE CITY HAS TO OFFER. With the births of their two children, Hugo, now seven, and Otto, five, the couple quickly realized the space didn't suit their needs quite so well, so spent time converting it into the beautiful but practical family home it is today.

GISELA'S JOB IS RUNNING THE UK ARM OF THE EXCITING AMERICAN FASHION, ACCESSORIES, AND HOMEWARE COMPANY ANTHROPOLOGIE, which exposes her to a wealth of creative talent from all over the world. SHE HAS A FANTASTIC EYE AND AN INNATE SENSE OF NEW AND EMERGING TRENDS, TOTALLY IN LINE WITH THE COMPANY'S PIONEERING ETHOS. She and her team have their finger well and truly on the pulse and are committed to using Anthropologie as a springboard to support and help the talented individuals whose work she champions. Her home is a clear reflection of this, filled with pieces by up-and-coming as well as established contemporary artists.

The bare brick walls give a real earthy look to the space, complementing the simple, original stone fireplace and contemporary gilt mirror.

Two framed original comic strips from the **1970s** hang low on the hallway wall for the children to see, just above a table made from parts of a reclaimed boat.

The huge circular metal bookcase from Anthropologie is both striking and useful, displaying family photographs, books, with practical as well as decorative bookends, and also art. The piece of painted wood in the center is by the Italian artist Nicola Bolla.

Filling this first-floor office space is an eclectic mixture of items bought over time from Anthropologie. A print of a phrenology head is propped up against an enormous abstract mural by the French artist Aurelie Alvarez. The canvas bag in front of the antique desk is by Leslie Oschmann, who was Anthropologie's visual director, from her Swarm collection.

INDIVIDUAL ECLECTICISM

3

The homes in this chapter illustrate perfectly how filling them with things that are loved and have meaning works so incredibly well. It is true to say that their owners are all professionals in the field of design and interiors, but it's plain to see there is nothing fixed or contrived about what they have done. Different patterns and textures, collections of fine and rough accessories from different decades, all sit happily together. The overall impression is both dramatic and intimate.

PUSHING THE BOUNDARIES

Shaun Clarkson is an interior designer, while husband Paul Brewster is a textile designer— a formidable duo when it came to renovating their central London Georgian home. Incredibly expressive men, they have both had long and illustrious careers in the world of interior design, largely in the hospitality business. Among many other London projects, Shaun has designed the Fifth Floor Bar at Harvey Nichols in Knightsbridge, the 10 Room bar, and the Raw Club—all garnering plaudits from the critics. The work he does often involves a riot of color and lots of glamour, such as the industry demands.

Their house, which is very typical of the Georgian period, was built in 1730 and has had a rather checkered past. Originally a dairy, it had for the last thirty years been an accountant's office until Shaun and Paul acquired it. THE BUILDING IS STEEPED IN HISTORY WITH LOTS OF SMALL, INTERESTING ROOMS OVER FOUR FLOORS, INCLUDING A BASEMENT. RENOVATING THE HOUSE HAS BEEN A REAL LABOR OF LOVE. As their work takes them all over the world and they are constantly on the move, this home needed to be an unconditional retreat where they could relax, unwind, and forget about their hectic schedules but still be close to their work.

↑ A neutral palette pervades in the study, centered around the marble fireplace, with a collection of white Hornsea china on the mantelpiece and a piece of art unearthed in a New York City flea market. The gray upholstered womb chair is by Knoll, while the starburst rug was specially made to Shaun and Paul's design and is available from their store.

◄◄ An original G Plan chair from the '60s has been covered with leftover "zebra" fabric from a commission at the Atlantic Bar and Grill restaurant in London. Although not original to the house, the fireplace came from another Georgian property nearby, so is exactly right for this sitting room.

◄◄ ◄◄ The soaring glass roof over this riotous living room has a calming influence so that the mix of colors, patterns, shapes, and textures doesn't overwhelm. The **1950s**-style wallpaper is from the work of an **American** retro designer, and the pattern is also used to cover the gigantic sofa. The huge pillows have been made from vintage **Dior** scarves. Behind the sofa is a beveled mirror in a zigzag design, which was a nightmare for the builders to install but it does look fantastic. The galleon ship from the **1940s** is of no particular design merit—it is purely decorative sitting on the '50s Italian coffee table with big black ball feet. Two **G Plan** chairs in a raspberry pink, also from the '50s, balance the space.

▷► Rather subdued compared with the rest of the house is the screening room, where **Shaun** and **Paul** can relax and read from the shelves of art books, or watch a movie or the television. Original **G Plan** armchairs, reupholstered by their own company **Pitfield**, are perfectly placed for relaxation either side of a vintage French lamp on top of a mid-**20**th-century, glass-topped coffee table. The shelves are also home to some of their collections of ceramics, including the large-scale retro pieces from Germany and the more delicate and finer English china of **Hornsea** and **Denby**. The original artwork on the left-hand wall is from a Christmas card made by **Paul**'s textiles tutor **Natalie Gibson** when he was a student at **Central Saint Martins**. **Paul** always speaks about her with great affection.

▰▸ The palette and pace of the study are less hectic than some other rooms in the house but nevertheless still adventurous. Making a sumptuous backdrop for the Pitfield white leather sofa bed is the wall of gold leaf line drawings by Shaun, depicting the open-plan loft apartment that was their previous home. Several African artifacts are dotted around the room, including an animal skin stretched over a drum, and a wicker and reeded lamp. The stripy rug was woven exclusively for them.

The couple have a lifestyle and interiors store, not too far from home, called Pitfield London, which helps feed their compulsion to collect. ALMOST EVERYTHING THEY FIND GOES TO THE STORE FIRST BUT, THEY CONFESS, ALL THE ATTENTION-GRABBING PIECES TEND TO END UP AT HOME. Many of the ideas that they nurtured for the house have become product staples sold in the store-reupholstered chairs, vintage Dior scarf cushions, and vintage wallpapers are all available to buy.

Shaun and Paul are also co-owners of boutique vacation retreats in Norfolk, England, called Cliff Barns and Carrington House, as well as a country home close by, where they love nothing more than relaxing in the house and tending the garden in summer.

In the screening room, a crystal chandelier floor lamp makes a sophisticated counterpoint to the amateur paintings. These are just two of the many portraits from the **1950s and '60s** that the couple have discovered at flea markets and turned into a collection.

This impressive wall light with turquoise shades was bought at a flea market and then carried home as hand luggage. The gilt eagle in flight is another particularly special find.

After living in a large, open-plan loft space with plain white walls, Shaun and Paul craved the coziness that they knew a Georgian house could offer them. To that end, they have filled their home with color and put back fireplaces that had been stripped out, creating lots of intimate nooks and corners.

To say that Shaun and Paul are obsessive collectors is an understatement. They love china, particularly bold mid-20th-century German and the relatively finer English Hornsea and Denby, and they have sizeable collections of both. THE 1950S AND '60S ARE PARTICULARLY APPEALING FOR THEM, AND OBJECTS FROM THOSE DECADES FILL THE HOUSE. THEY ARE BIG FANS OF ERCOL AND G PLAN FURNITURE, WHICH WERE BOTH VERY INFLUENTIAL IN THEIR TIME, but they prefer to reupholster their pieces and breathe new life into them, giving them a completely rare quality.

Hunting for new treasures at secondhand stores and flea markets forms a big part of Shaun and Paul's weekends-you only have to peek in their kitchen cupboards to see the extent of their searching. Many of the individual pieces they have found for the house work incredibly well, such as the old leaded glass library doors that greet you on entering the house. They are the perfect addition to the hallway and look as if they have always belonged there.

THE KITCHEN AREA HAS ALL THE OBVIOUS MODERN FITTINGS TO MAKE ENTERTAINING, COOKING, AND CLEANING EASY BUT THAT'S WHERE ANY CONFORMITY ENDS. TRUE TO STYLE, YOU ARE SUDDENLY TAKEN BY SURPRISE-on the small Georgian pedestal dining table opposite there is an enormous Victorian dome filled with stuffed birds, a present from Paul to Shaun.

Entertaining plays a large role in the couple's life, and they love to cook for friends. Evenings usually start with everyone chatting together in the kitchen/diner, while cooking is under way but after eating, they invariably end up in the glass-roofed living room "spinning the decks" with their disco music or watching a movie in the screening room.

↑ , ⌖→ At the opposite end from the working part of the kitchen is this cozy and convivial space. The pedestal table is original Georgian while the chairs, covered in a beautiful turquoise leather, are original G Plan from the 1960s. Crowning it all is a huge antler light, which took plenty of time and careful maneuvering to get through the leaded glass doors. The picture above the fireplace was a free download from Gilbert and George when the artists appeared on British television's South Bank Show in 2007.

↑, ←◻ The crystal chandelier makes the perfect grand statement to visitors to this extraordinary home. Equally impressive are the leaded glass library doors reflected in the glass of the many framed photographs and art that line the walls. This disciplined display, set against a plain blue wall with the pictures neatly and evenly placed, continues up the stairs to the landing, increasing its overall impact.

Collections are very important to Shaun and Paul, and they account for much of the display in their home. THE HALLWAY, STAIRCASE, AND LANDING, WITH THE HIGH-SIDED WALLS, ARE THE PERFECT PLACE TO HANG AN IMPRESSIVE COLLECTION OF BLACK-AND-WHITE PHOTOGRAPHS AND PAINTINGS THAT HAVE BEEN AMASSED OVER THE YEARS TO MAKE AN IMPACTFUL STATEMENT. ALTHOUGH OF DIFFERENT SHAPES, SIZES, AND SUBJECT MATTER, THE PICTURES ARE ALL IN BLACK FRAMES, WHICH SERVE TO UNITE THEM. The leaded glass door and fanlight above, once part of a municipal library, together with the elegant crystal chandelier, create just the right kind of entrance to this gallery.

Some collections remain out of sight, though. The couple's creative imaginations are also revealed in how they dress, and they have devised big walk-in closets in their dressing room to house their enviable collections of bold statement clothes.

The couple's love of the unexpected continues throughout all the rooms in the house, including the master bedroom and bathroom, where different styles rub shoulders easily with one another. In the bedroom, THE PANELED WALLS AND DOORS HAVE BEEN LOVINGLY RESTORED TO THEIR GEORGIAN SPLENDOR, BUT THE DECORATION IS MUCH MORE CONTEMPORARY. The bathroom, meanwhile, is more art deco in style, with a bold geometric pattern of yellow and white tiles on the walls and complementary fittings, accompanied by metal wall art from the '60s and a vintage gilt chandelier.

This house has so many ideas that could easily be borrowed. I think it also proves, once again, that mixing styles and periods is the best way to be the most expressive in your home. If you love it, do it!

◄◄ In the master bedroom, a piece of **1960s** metal wall art by **Curtis Jeré** hangs over the deep-buttoned, duck-egg-blue headboard. Similarly tactile is the heavily embroidered Chinese silk bedcover. Combined, these elements create a very calm and restful space, while losing none of the unexpected design ethos of the rest of the home.

►► The yellow and white bathroom tiles are by **Moderna**, laid in a striking geometric pattern. More metallic wall art by **Curtis Jeré** adorns the walls, while a vintage gilt chandelier is the perfect partner to the art.

▼ A huge and heavy dark wood mirror adds contrast to the tiles but does not look out of place in the slightest.

Mixing styles and periods is the best way to be the most expressive in your home

←◧ Creating an unusual filter of light and providing privacy at the living room window are these really clever blinds. They are made from pieces of wood hinged together, so they fold back, with the raw edges barely touching. A simple gilt hook is an inspired fastening.

↑ Carefully arranged but mismatching pieces of furniture work well together, filling the living room and creating a comfortable and convivial space. The sofa and armchairs are all old but restored and reupholstered by Clarke & Reilly. These interior designers have a nostalgic aesthetic and use interesting combinations of fabric. The two low-level, carved-back chairs are from Ethiopia. On the back of the sofa are two cushions from Squint.

RAW BEAUTY

I first met Joel Bernstein on the day we photographed his London home. The house summed up exactly what I wanted to bring to my readers–it is the perfect example of a Creative Space with no rules and no boundaries. I have since learnt that Joel simply restores and renovates houses as a hobby, and that he no longer lives here. At first, I was disappointed but then, I thought, there would be more houses in the future with his handwriting, no doubt different but equally fantastic.

THERE ARE MANY THINGS I WOULD LIKE TO BORROW FROM JOEL AND THIS HOUSE IN TERMS OF IDEAS AND INSPIRATIONS. I LOVE THE RAWNESS OF THE SPACE. It is beautifully finished and comfortable but the materials and the style are earthy and raw. Inspiration comes from his native South Africa but also from the time when he was head of concept at Liberty of London, the quirky department store.

With his partner Walid al Damirji, Joel now co-owns Cocomaya, a chocolate café in several London locations. The concept is both groundbreaking and innovative, and the cafés are all simple but beautiful.

THE HOUSE IS PART OF A TERRACED OR ROW HOUSE COMMUNITY IN NORTHWEST LONDON, KNOWN AS QUEENS PARK ESTATE, WHICH WAS BUILT IN AROUND 1874 FOR ARTISANS AND RAILWAY WORKERS. AN IMPORTANT EXAMPLE OF SOCIAL HOUSING AT THE TIME, THE ESTATE WAS DESIGNED IN THE GOTHIC REVIVAL STYLE, and embellished with a variety of architectural details such as turrets, pinnacles, gables, and arches. Today, a diverse cross section of people lives on the estate, and all the houses have white exterior woodwork. Joel is very hands-on and always gets involved in every aspect of a building project, selecting materials and working with builders who

◀◀◀ ▶ A rusty table hosts a selection of precious items that Joel has collected over the years. Everything, from the silver box to the semi-precious stones and seashells, has been placed with absolute care. The focus of the display is the classical bust from James Plumb, the design duo of Hannah Plumb and James Russell. A delicate leaf design has been beautifully etched all over, giving the bust new life and a rare quality.

Everything on display has been positioned precisely, highlighting their individual importance to the owner

understand his vision and can help him realize it. Inside, the house is typical of the period, with small but compact rooms, but Joel opened up the whole of the downstairs so the rooms flow from one to the other.

➔ Typical of Joel's eclectic style is the combination of a solid wood "trestle" table and a rather delicate antique chair, shown in the space that bridges the living room and the kitchen. Leaning against the recessed shelving units, home to Joel's fascinating collection of art books, shells, and various other treasures, is a vintage fruit ladder. Tucked away behind the wall is a really unusual table, from Clarke & Reilly, with white legs that resemble tree roots. Leather storage boxes in different sizes act as an interesting plinth for the phalaenopsis orchid and glass bottle. In stark contrast to all the decorative objects are two bare, industrial-style light bulbs.

Further along on the ground floor is this redundant fireplace, now a convenient home for a mid-20th-century desk lamp. The two 16th-century chairs are unexpected companions, and bring a slight majesty to the space. The artwork in the rough wooden frame, made from tiny colored tiles, is by **R**uth Elliot. A selection of very collectible ceramics by Hylton Nel, the **S**outh **A**frican potter, painter, and sculptor, is displayed on the open shelving unit.

Beneath these two highly individual
pieces of vintage art, with their
comical mislabeling, are two
cushions by Squint, a British textile
company, famous for its exuberant
and bespoke home accessories—
I would expect nothing less from
Joel in his home. They are a jolly
addition against the plain white,
paneled wood walls.

◄◄ The open-plan kitchen, which has been extended to open out onto the garden, has been specially made for Joel. His love of raw wood is very much in evidence. The cabinets have all been treated with a dark stain, which gives a really earthy quality, but the kitchen still has all the trappings of an efficient workspace. Patterned glazed tiles make a pretty splashback behind the modern, stainless-steel stove.

Joel loves wood, and it appears as a finish in many parts of the decoration, from raw wooden shutters, which are simply pulled together by a small gilt hook, to the slatted wood wall in the bedroom. In the living room, the wood-paneled walls are painted white, while in the bespoke kitchen, they are covered in a dark stain.

Like so many of the homeowners featured in this book, JOEL HAS A SKILLFUL EYE AND A SINGLE VISION. THE HOUSE IS FULL OF UNUSUAL FURNITURE, FURNISHINGS, AND DECORATIVE OBJECTS THAT HE HAS DISCOVERED, BOTH AT HOME AND ABROAD. There are antiques, contemporary pottery, unusual upholstered chairs, Moroccan rugs, Ethiopian chairs -the list is endless, and his natural creative instinct is to put them all together to achieve a wholly unique living space.

Joel knows no boundaries when it comes to art and design. He has a particular fondness for South African art, and has included quite a few pieces from his homeland here. Above the dining table is an abstract watercolor by Irma Stern. Collections of pottery by Hylton Nel, now a very collectible ceramist from Cape Town, are also dotted around the house.

JOEL HAS A BRAVE AND CLEVER WAY WITH FURNITURE, COMPLETELY IGNORING ACCEPTED PEARLS OF WISDOM WHEN IT COMES TO THEIR PLACEMENT. He has English antiques, for example, sitting next to carved wood chairs from Ethiopia. He is not afraid to use color either, and mixes fabrics and patterns, creating unlikely but hugely successful alliances.

Striking out with confidence has given this space a rare quality

Facing the stove is this simple, raw
wood dining table, surrounded by
several different old kitchen chairs.
Hanging over the table is an Irma
Stern painting. Joel has no television
but enjoys listening to his Roberts
Radio, especially while he is cooking.

Moving upstairs to the landing, the simple, black-painted handrail and bare, industrial-style light bulb are typical of Joel's decorating style.

Exposed copper pipes are like a frame running around the tiny, original hand basin. Hanging alongside is an oversized hammam towel. A cluster of vintage handheld mirrors makes a delightful alternative to one larger, conventional mirror.

Joel's bed is covered with a gorgeous, glittery Moroccan wedding blanket, a glamorous counterpoint to the slatted wood wall. Joel hand-picked every single piece of wood for the wall to give it the desired random and color-mismatch look.

The upstairs of the house contains two bedrooms and a bathroom. THE MASTER BEDROOM HAS WOOD-LINED WALLS AND DOUBLE DOORS. THESE ARE BESPOKE, SIMPLE IN DESIGN, AND MADE FROM UNTREATED WOOD. SIMPLE GILT CATCHES ARE USED AS FASTENINGS. Covering the bed is a ceremonial marriage blanket from Morocco. Just off the bedroom is Joel's private bathroom, complete with a roll-top bathtub, a circular brass shower curtain rail, and a basin in the corner. All the bathroom fixtures are Victorian but with up-to-date plumbing. In places, Joel has plumbed in 19th-century faucets and used exposed copper pipes to give the space an air of authenticity.

In the guest bedroom, a Victorian floral hand basin, on an aged metal stand, is surrounded by exposed copper pipes, some of them covered in verdigris. A white table acts as a dressing table with the carved Ethiopian chair. Giving a blast of color and modernity is the quirky piece of art by Henry Villiers. Yet another bare, industrial-style bulb lights the way.

➨ There's no shortage of wood even in Joel's bathroom, with the floor-to-ceiling cupboards and dark brown floorboards. The black-painted, roll-top tub suits the age of the house perfectly.

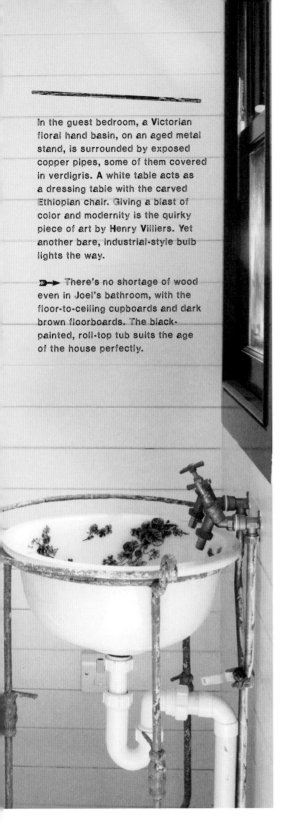

There is even more wood paneling in the guest room, but here it runs horizontally and has been painted white. In keeping with the age of the house, Joel has installed a small Victorian sink unit for authenticity but then he accompanied it with a curved-back, rustic chair from Ethiopia and a modern piece of art by Henry Villiers. Quite a mix! Indeed, I HAVE RARELY SEEN A HOUSE WHERE THE OWNER HAS RUN WITH SO MANY REALLY DIFFERENT IDEAS, COMBINED THEM TOGETHER IN SUCH A CONFIDENT WAY, and created the most powerful and spectacular interior.

◄◄ Personal mementoes decorate the entire house. On the living room wall hangs an original poster for the movie "Top Hat," a gift from David to Martin when he appeared in the London West End stage version. The John Derian decoupage plate, with vivid blue cornflowers, was David's leaving present from colleagues at Selfridges, which is where we met. Similarly, the carriage clock on top of the Arts and Crafts fire surround once belonged to David's Popa, who was given it when he retired.

TREADING THE BOARDS

This beautifully restored period property in northwest London is the home of David Walker-Smith, Martin McCarthy, and Ella, the cockapoo. Martin, a musical theater actor, and David, a retail executive and enthusiastic amateur actor, have created A SUBTLE AND REFINED HOME FILLED WITH DESIGN CLASSICS. ANTIQUES MARKETS, LOCAL SECONDHAND STORES, AND EBAY HAVE ALL YIELDED A RICH SELECTION OF FINDS that suit their home and their personalities down to the ground.

DECORATING CHOICES ARE BOLD BUT UNDERSTATED, AND THE HOUSE HASN'T BEEN FILLED JUST FOR THE SAKE OF IT. The couple have placed a great deal of importance on including objects that have emotional significance for them, things that have been passed down through their families. These give their home an incredible warmth and intimacy.

When David and Martin bought the house, it was a shadow of its former self, but THEIR PAINSTAKING RENOVATION HAS GIVEN IT BACK ITS INTEGRITY. They were lucky to find that all the original floorboards were still in place. Now repaired and reconditioned, they make a striking statement. Other original features, such as cornices and moldings, have been carefully restored, too.

◄◄ The newly upholstered **1950s** chairs are unfussy additions to this corner of the living room. The diminutive granddaughter clock, given to David's grandparents in the **1930s** as a wedding present, has enormous sentimental value.

↑ Splashes of yellow from the silk cushion and original occasional table—an unbelievable find at a flea market—and the blue of the '50s armchair are eye-catching color combinations. The words on the John Derian decoupage plate sum up the decor of this home very simply: "Things I like"!

▶▶ The bright, through living room, with all the original cornicing, is painted in a pale, neutral shade that tones down the effect of the white wooden shutters. Hanging from the ceiling is a slatted cedarwood lamp from the Finnish company Secto Design. Two gray-fabric, mid-20th-century-style sofas and a sage-green, silk-mix rug are simple but comfortable additions.

A MAGPIE'S EYE

◄◄ The bedroom wall is covered with pictures and photographs of religious figures collected on Nicky's travels. In this shrine to all faiths, made even more evocative by the flickering tea lights, Our Lady of Guadalupe plays center stage, surrounded by Hindu gods, gurus, sacred hearts, and other icons from temples and churches.

➤➤ This snapshot of the living room reveals many of the original features typical of the apartment, such as the high ceiling, elaborate cornicing, and grand marble fireplace. The original wooden shutters are left half open for privacy, at the same time allowing light to filter in from outside.

Nicky Butler was born with a magpie's eye, an essential ingredient for a designer whose jewelry creations sell all over the world. Forty five years ago, he and Simon Wilson launched their eponymous shop in London: Butler & Wilson. The brand, loved by stars and royalty alike, has become an international success, with its jewelry collections coveted by magazines for their top fashion shoots. NICKY NOW WORKS ALONE AND SPENDS MUCH OF HIS TIME TRAVELING IN HIS SEARCH FOR OLD AND NEW, HEART-STOPPING, AND EXOTIC STONES TO USE ON HIS DESIGNS which he sells on HSN. He knows what women want to wear and, with this in mind, is on a constant quest to bring back something original and exciting for them. Along the way, he has collected homes from places as diverse as Miami, Hollywood, Jaipur, and, of course, his native London. Featured here is his beautifully stuccoed apartment in an Italianate Victorian villa in west London.

A low bookcase, which runs the length of one living room wall, allows the splendid double doors with all their original moldings to remain unshadowed. The oil on canvas above the shelves is by Nicky's artist friend Richard Nott. Balancing the display at either end is a ceramic peacock from 1928 and a bronze statue by Gustave Miklos.

THIS FIRST-FLOOR APARTMENT IS HUGE WITH HIGH CEILINGS AND WELL-PROPORTIONED, SPACIOUS ROOMS. Those at the front look out over the quiet leafy street. Nicky's bedroom at the back has views of the communal gardens. Hidden behind tall hedges is the busy main road leading into central London-you would never guess that, though, as it's so peaceful.

Nicky has had this apartment for over 25 years and it is his bolt-hole whenever he is in London. Built at the end of the 19th century, and typical of the style of the period, it has large bay windows with original shutters, all the original cornicing, and period features. WALLS PAINTED IN A NEUTRAL SHADE GIVE NICKY FREE REIN TO ADD HIS COLLECTIONS OF ART, CERAMICS, AND BOOKS.

In my last book, **CREATIVE DISPLAY**, we featured Nicky's Hollywood home, which is filled to the brim with diverse religious icons. In this London home, Nicky has filled an entire wall with religious memorabilia, all of which have personal significance. Another themed collection is displayed in the hallway. Bold, graphic posters from the 1920s of the exotic dancer Josephine Baker cover the wall with barely an inch between them, inviting the visitor to scrutinize each one.

◀◀ Paintings and posters, including many by the French artist **Paul Colin** of Josephine Baker from the **1920s**, jostle for space on this wall in the hallway outside Nicky's bedroom. A framed photographic collage of friends and family adds to this interesting collection.

In this carefully curated display, elements from nature share the console table with beautiful manmade pieces. Perching in front of some petrified wood from the prow of a canoe is a stuffed crow, alongside a contemporary glass vase by Kate Hume and a chrome candleholder from Georg Jensen. The "sword" of a swordfish is a counterbalance to the elegant glass altar vase of dried branches.

➤➤ Soothing and monochrome, like the rest of the apartment, is the guest bedroom with two charcoal drawings of dresses by Richard hanging on the wall.

SEASIDE ADVENTURE FOR FASHION DUO

Richard Nott and Graham Fraser founded the innovative fashion label Workers for Freedom in the 1980s. Life then was frantic, all about schedules and deadlines, but since selling the company in 2000, the pace has slowed down considerably. THEY MOVED OUT OF LONDON, EVENTUALLY ENDING UP ON THE ENGLISH SOUTH COAST, WHERE THEY NOW LIVE AN ALTOGETHER MORE PEACEFUL AND RELAXED LIFE, with their dog Albert, a cavapoo. Walking Albert every day by the ocean or on the South Downs is a ritual that brings both robust health and a clear mind, so that they can enjoy the things that make them thrive. The apartment they share is a reflection of this new-found peace, as well as their relaxed style.

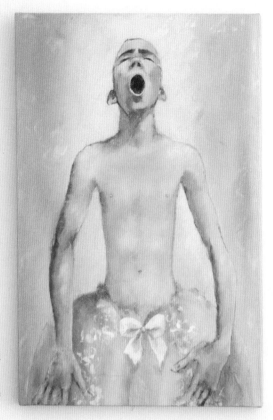

Now that there is peace in their lives, as well as time, Richard has returned to one of his loves: painting. He works from a studio just a short walk away from their apartment. Graham, meanwhile, has immersed himself in the cultural community and uses his business skills to help support and drive art and cultural exhibitions and events in the town.

After leaving the fashion industry, Richard and Graham became custodians of a large National Trust house, Stoneacre in Kent. As well as making it more contemporary and relevant to today's living, they became passionate gardeners, well known for their open-minded and revolutionary approach, just as they had been in the fashion world. Although seemingly very different, GARDENS ARE LIKE FASHION, NEEDING CONSTANT HARD WORK, A CLEAR EYE FOR COLOR AND DETAIL, AND THE ABILITY TO PUSH BOUNDARIES AND NOT ALWAYS DO WHAT IS EXPECTED!

The magical touch that the boys bestowed on the National Trust house and garden is clearly evident in their apartment, although on a smaller scale. They have made it simple, light, and airy, and full of treasures collected over the years.

Pieces of art are displayed throughout the apartment. One of Richard's more recent pieces, an arresting oil on canvas of a shouting man, is displayed above the cabinet in the master bedroom. Propped up against the wall is an original pen-and-ink drawing of Picasso by Cecil Beaton, signed and particularly precious, alongside a contemporary lamp with a retro shade. The small collection of stone and pottery vessels was chosen simply for color, feel, and diversity.

The decorating style that Richard and Graham adopted from the start was all about creating comfort and warmth against a blank canvas. WITH NO COMPETING COLORS AND TEXTURES TO CONTEND WITH, THE DISPLAYS CAN BE EASILY CHANGED AND THE SPACES RE-INVENTED WITH NEW PIECES OF ART.

Entertaining is one of their favorite pastimes. Richard and Graham both like to cook and experiment with different cuisines, and the dining experience accordingly takes on many different guises. When serving colorful, spicy cuisine, out come the bright plates, tablecloth, and napkins. For a more sophisticated affair, as shown here, VINTAGE GLASSWARE AND PLAIN WHITE PLATES DECORATE A WHITE LINEN TABLECLOTH, SO THAT THE SETTING RESEMBLES SOMETHING LIKE A DUTCH 17TH-CENTURY STILL-LIFE OIL PAINTING. I am so grateful that my previous job in the fashion industry allowed me to meet Richard and Graham and become such good friends. Even though they have moved away from London, their apartment is really only a short journey away for me and I am still able to enjoy their generous hospitality.

➡ The large, airy kitchen is the setting for many dinner parties and casual suppers. Even though the long table is set for an informal lunch, it is laid with a French linen tablecloth, albeit un-ironed, a selection of vintage carafes and decanters, white linen napkins, and silver cutlery. An oil painting by Richard of an embroidered dress hangs on the wall. Making an unlikely but perfect match are the clay pigeon and white ceramic pitcher on the window ledge.

CAREFULLY CURATED PURISTS

In all of these homes, the owners have paid close attention to the style or design that they originally pursued and are now preserving it through careful management. Never wavering from the path, they have mastered the overall desired effect and maintained a correctness through their choice of color, finish, period, and design detail. To curate in this way is close to being a museum curator, where the selection and placement of every item is carefully considered and controlled. The overall effect is both calming and serene. Typically, a lot of white or shades of white and cream are central to the look.

KEEPING TIME

↑ , ← The beautifully worn glass mercury mirror in the living room reflects the time-worn nature of the space. Either side is an early portrait and a vintage seascape hanging in the old-fashioned way from metal picture hangers. Three sofas, one deep-buttoned with mismatching cushions, the other two in raw natural linen and decorated with stitched Indian throws, give off a bohemian air. The unusual occasional table has turned cotton reel legs. On top sits a wooden hat mold purely for decoration.

I was thrilled when John Derian agreed to have his Manhattan home featured in this book. HIS APARTMENT REALLY IS A BEAUTIFUL SPACE, TAKING UP THE WHOLE OF THE FIRST FLOOR OF AN 1850S BUILDING THAT WAS PREVIOUSLY A GARMENT FACTORY. John rents the dilapidated apartment from a sculptor who had lived there since the 1960s. He has restored it to make it comfortable for everyday living, while retaining all the original features and, in most cases, the original patina. It has a well-balanced shape, and there is light coming in from all sides.

Reflected in the pockmarked mirror
behind are an old artist's testing
board and one of the many table
lamps that contribute to the relaxing
feel. Cushions made from an eclectic
mix of fabrics, including an old kilim
and ticking, are scattered casually
on the sofas. The glass of water
on the tray is for Skip, John's
elderly cat, to drink from.

↑ Still in the living room, a daybed with loose, white cotton covers and a selection of cushions, is where John likes to sit and look out onto the gardens below. Adding to the comfort is a footstool fashioned from an old army rucksack and a large chunk of wood used as a table.

⟹ Old chairs, renovated and upholstered in pale linen, surround the raw wood dining table. The pot on top with remarkably lifelike, hand-crafted paper flowers is by Livia Cetti. Above the original paneled dado is a piece of hand-painted 18th-century wallpaper.

↑ **More undressed sash windows fill the room with light.** An intricate tangle of dried wood decorates the top of the cabinet, which is crammed with found objects. Sitting on the old table are a myrtle bush and an old artist's testing board, seen earlier reflected in the mirror.

➤ **A closer look at the tall, glass-fronted cabinet** reveals stacks of mismatched plates, cake stands, bowls, and silverware, all jumbled together with pieces from the French ceramist **Astier de Villatte**— an altogether pleasing display.

➤➤ **This magnificent cabinet of treasures** includes coral and shells alongside glassware, mercury vases, and other small ornaments.

Cabinets filled to the brim with intriguing found objects convey the feel of a museum

The apartment is just a few short paces away from John's workshop, where he makes his gorgeous glass decoupage plates. John started his company in 1989 and has attracted a huge band of loyal followers. HIS WORK IS SHOWCASED AT THE NEW YORK INTERNATIONAL GIFT FAIR, WHICH IS WHERE WE MET. I AM ONE OF HIS BIGGEST FANS AND MAKE A BEELINE FOR HIS STORES EACH TIME I VISIT THE CITY. He works closely with European artists and also sells a mixture of eclectic decorative items in his two stores. I have featured his decoupage plates in my previous books, so I was keen to include his home here. John has lived in this apartment for less than a year but it is obvious that the apparently casual way in which he has furnished and decorated it is nothing of the sort. It is all very carefully curated, with not a single jarring note.

◄═► In the kitchen, a large, one-of-a-kind Robert Ogden light hangs low from the ceiling, the six bulbs beneath the round reflective shade giving a warm glow. A close-up of the countertop reveals a collection of old wooden chopping boards, handsome as well as practical.

◄═ Tucked in alongside the bedroom is the unexpected office space, filled with books, pictures, decorative objects, and old boxes. Double wooden shutters, original to the building, shield the room from the afternoon sun. With the wall taken back to the brickwork and no hint of modern technology, the room feels steeped in history. A quirky ceiling lamp, hanging precariously from a long metal pole, directs light onto the busy desk.

═► A long, narrow room leads from the entrance hallway into the living room. Shelf upon shelf of books, magazines, and old boxes runs the length and height of an entire wall. Lined up along the bottom is a charming collection of vintage children's chairs. A French crystal chandelier adds light and glamour.

I am really impressed by the way John has incorporated old and retired objects into his home, adding to the sense of history that already exists. HE THROWS VINTAGE TEXTILES AND KILIMS OVER SOFAS AND COFFEE TABLES TO SOFTEN THEIR HARD EDGES, AND FILLS THE APARTMENT TO THE BRIM WITH WONDERFUL FINDS. HE HAS THE ENVIABLE ABILITY TO CREATE EXQUISITE STILL-LIFE MOMENTS.

The apartment offers many surprises. Next to the bedroom is a door behind which you'd expect to find a closet. In fact, it opens onto John's office space. Very much in keeping with the rest of the apartment, there is no evidence of 21st-century technology, although I was assured it existed but was just hidden from view.

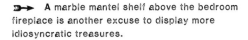

➤➤ A marble mantel shelf above the bedroom fireplace is another excuse to display more idiosyncratic treasures.

◄☰ Squeezed into the space between the entrance hall and the living room is a 19th-century Italian theater backdrop depicting a tall, classical-style cabinet stacked with boxes and journals. In front is a neat linen sofa, creating a memorable vignette. The worn and flaking paint on the narrow floorboards matches the color of the sofa. Another one-of-a-kind Robert Ogden light hangs from the ceiling.

➤➤ The "makeshift" fireplace in the hall leading to John's home office—the metal fireplace, originally sited in the bedroom, was leaning in the hallway during the renovations; John thought it looked so good that he had the contractor fix it there permanently. Above is a wonderful collection of art, from Hugo Guinness, Paul Lee, Deborah Boardman, and Agnes Barley.

I LOVE SEEING WHAT OBJECTS OTHER PEOPLE SEEK OUT AND COLLECT DURING THE COURSE OF THEIR LIVES AND HOW THEY WORK THEM INTO THEIR HOMES. JOHN TRAVELS A LOT FOR HIS WORK, AND THE JOURNEYS HE TAKES ALWAYS INSPIRE HIM and open his mind to distant cultures and other artisans' work. Closer to home is John's weekend retreat in Cape Cod, where there is more space to relax and recharge his batteries after the pace of the city. He is able to satisfy his magpie instinct here, too.

The chunky form of the original, low-level radiator contrasts with the very delicate vintage chair alongside. The chair has been newly upholstered in cream linen, while the cover tucked into the end of the spindly metal-framed bed is made of white cotton.

➤➤ An upturned, zinc water tank has a new lease of life as the most imaginative and effective bedside table. On top, a wooden mushroom lends a raw, decorative touch, while the twisted and gilded wooden lamp base adds glamour.

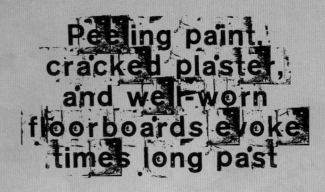

Peeling paint,
cracked plaster,
and well-worn
floorboards evoke
times long past

Folding wooden shutters in the
main bedroom block out the sun and
noise from the street below. The
original, raw wooden floorboards
and soft, creamy walls give the
space an overall softness and
unique charm. The old wooden
table by the bed is home to another
collection of precious found objects
and, of course, another glass of
water for Skip. A small, delicate
crystal chandelier hangs from
the ceiling.

Opposite the bedroom windows stands a battered chest of drawers. Displayed on top is a jumble of more favorite objects, including a paisley-decorated hat box and family photographs. An old oil on canvas portrait graces the wall. To the right of the doorway is an upholstered, semicircular sofa from Paris. There is a second sofa out of shot, but the two together would make a full circle.

◄─◖ Except for the original dark-stained floorboards, this gracious and light-filled living room is an homage to white. Beautiful original paneled walls, a stunning marble fireplace, French doors opening out onto the garden—all these elements create a quiet serenity. Although modern, the long sofa, with a gray cashmere throw over one arm, is at perfect ease among all these impressive architectural features. Not to be outdone or overlooked, **Pucci** has placed herself center stage on Joey's skateboard.

SEEKING AND FINDING PERFECTION

Katie and Gino da'Prato live with their two children Talia and Joey, and Pucci, the Pomeranian, in this absolutely gorgeous Georgian house of immense architectural merit. Set among eight acres of land in the Hertfordshire countryside, it boasts no less than ten fireplaces, all of them in working order, and eight bedrooms. THE QUIET AND RURAL SETTING MAKES IT PERFECT FOR BRINGING UP CHILDREN.

I FIRST MET KATIE WHEN WE WERE BOTH FASHION BUYERS. WE TRAVELED ALL OVER EUROPE TOGETHER, going to the shows and at the same time taking in all the beauty and culture that presented itself along the way. At the time, we took this all a bit for granted but now I realize how much actually rubbed off on us. The memories of grand opera houses, amazing châteaux, ballrooms, old cinemas-the list is endless-were unparalleled references to draw on when creating our own homes.

The tall double glass doors that open out onto the garden make this beautiful, long room incredibly light and airy. At one end, narrow folding screens, which almost reach the ceiling, are covered in damask wallpaper offering a relief against the plain wall. With smart but comfortable upholstered furniture arranged symmetrically, tonal cushions, and arrangements of small white flowers on the coffee table, the look is streamlined, unfussy, and welcoming.

Although no longer working in the fashion industry, Katie is still a perfectionist, which I'm sure drives Gino mad! But look at the result. I know that creating this home has been a labor of love, and there was an incredible amount of restoration work to be done before the family was able to move in. Katie has to be admired for her unflinching pursuit of exactly the right designs and color choices. I would love to count just how many shades of white exist in this home. If anyone ever thought that there was only one, this certainly disproves it!

What, for me, makes this house so incredibly special is how Katie has restored it to its former grandeur but at the same time has created a happy and relaxed home that her boisterous children enjoy, too. A lot of this is down to Katie and Gino's laid-back attitude to life but also to the fact that there is nothing in the home that is too precious to be touched or there just for show.

An entrance hall is always an indicator of what the rest of a house will look like and, on entering this room, you quickly realize that you are in for a treat. All the original features—from the cornices and architraves to the paneled doors and marble fireplace—have been expertly restored. Painted and decorated in various shades of white, as elsewhere, the space exudes peace and calm. A contemporary light hangs over an antique pedestal table, with a silver bowl containing, of course, white flowers. Three black-and-white photographs of a young ballerina hang above the paneled wainscot.

Some of the internal doors, as well as those overlooking the garden, are glass-paneled, welcoming in the sunlight. These doors, which lead from the family living room into the small parlor used for lunches, have an unusual decorative filter, which allows some privacy but doesn't restrict the light. An ornate chandelier adds a glamorous quality, as does the exquisite marble fireplace.

When Katie and Gino found this house, it must have been a "light bulb" moment. They instinctively knew that, although down at the heels and in desperate need of care and attention, it could be restored to its former beauty and become the home they dreamed of for their future, with the walled garden becoming the perfect protected outdoor play area for their children.

The upstairs rooms are just as white, beautiful, and immaculately restored as those downstairs. The ceilings are almost as high, the architectural detailing still in place. Even the original floorboards, covered with a dark stain as elsewhere, have survived the passing centuries.

↑ Peeking through into the master bedroom, one can see Katie tidying the contemporary four-poster bed, its dark wood complementing the floorboards. Talia and Joey are sprawled out on the bed, although only Joey's feet are visible. It's a typical relaxed family scene where nothing is out of the ordinary except, that is, for the amazing surroundings.

Adopting a style like this, even on a small scale is all about discipline

These rooms are also thoughtfully furnished, with not a single rogue element or any extraneous clutter in sight to spoil the effect. Traditional mixes with contemporary but so expertly that nothing appears out of place.

Beneath the window of the en-suite master bathroom, with a view of the garden below, stands a traditional roll-top bathtub. How soothing it must be to bathe in this space! Although contemporary, the clear acrylic Philippe Starck Ghost chairs either side of the tub have a sophistication that complements the traditional elements. Silver fabric cushions on top add a touch of glamour. A small chrome decorative table holds a posy of white roses and a scented candle ready to burn.

◄─ Double doors off the living room lead to a small balcony high above the busy street. The view is of the treetops, which adds to the tranquility of the space. The Berber rug, bought while on holiday in **Morocco**, is surrounded by design classics: a stunning **Maarten Visser Slaapbank** sofa, a chrome and glass round table from **Eileen Gray**, and a **Marcel Breuer** chair in the corner next to an **Alvar Aalto Artek** stool.

LEAVING NOTHING TO CHANCE

There is nothing accidental about this home. Debby Kuypers and Reza Schuster, who are both architects, have a clear and shared vision of how they want to live, and their beautiful but compact London apartment reflects this. Set in a post-war housing estate of immense architectural merit, THEIR HOME IS A VISUAL FEAST, WITH ITS CAREFULLY CHOSEN PIECES OF DESIGNER FURNITURE, BUT IT IS ALSO EMINENTLY PRACTICAL. THEIR TRAINED EYE AND EXPERIENCE HAVE ENSURED THAT THE SPACE IS WELL DESIGNED BUT ALSO COMFORTABLE AND SERENE, suiting them and their busy lives, as well as their young daughter Minna.

A home can always be made to feel peaceful, regardless of what is going on outside

← Daughter Minna sits playing in her **Artek** highchair, oblivious to the designer delights around her. **Mart Stam** tubular steel and leather chairs push neatly under the plain wooden table when not in use. **A Best & Lloyd lamp** takes up little space on the parquet floor, which was carefully laid in a **1950s** style in keeping with the age and design of the apartment.

↓ As with all the other rooms, the bathroom is functional and easy to maintain without sacrificing any design quality. A **Mondaine Swiss** railway clock hangs on the white-painted wall; a **Roberts** radio sits on the uncluttered window ledge for listening to during relaxing baths.

Juggling work and childcare isn't easy, especially when lives are so busy, like Debby and Reza's. However, I have learned from experience that having a small, well-organized but comfortable home comes halfway to meeting the challenge, and this is exactly what we have here. The well-chosen pieces in the apartment are all very practical and design-led, while storage is generous, so that everything has its place, including Minna's toys. THE COLOR PALETTE IS WARM AND INVITING, WHICH GIVES THE HOME A REAL FEELING OF CALM, in spite of it being in a block of apartments in a busy part of London. The apartment's position among the trees gives a sense of being somewhere else, somewhere peaceful. The integrity of the architect's vision remains, and the fact that Debby and Reza choose to live here is a testament to the original vision.

Even though the space in the long, narrow kitchen is limited, the couple have designed it so that every spare inch has been exploited. When not in use, pots and pans are hidden away behind fitted, floor-to-ceiling wall cabinets. Even this most practical room of the home sports a number of designer pieces: a chrome Best & Lloyd wall lamp sets the tone as it illuminates the stove and work surface, while an Alvar Aalto Artek stool stands beneath the shelf displaying a Stelton coffee set and a Dualit toaster. The single mixer tap is by Vola.

↑ An ornate Capodimonte pitcher, with a large, curved handle and a delicate body embellished with fine ceramic flowers, has been sprayed with matte black paint by Diana.

←€ A collection of vintage retro china, contemporary candlesticks and candles, and other favored objects has also had the matte black paint treatment from Diana. Set against the exposed brick wall and wooden mantelpiece, both painted a stark white, they make an impressive statement.

After time spent living in Munich, Germany, then in the UK, where they are from originally, George and Diana Sharp moved to New York City with their son Joe. That was eight years ago. George is a fashion designer, while Diana used to work with Vidal Sassoon. THE DECISION TO LIVE IN NEW YORK WAS DOWN TO GEORGE'S WORK. HE HAS CARVED AN ILLUSTRIOUS CAREER WORKING FOR THE BEST FASHION HOUSES IN THE WORLD. ALTHOUGH THE HOURS ARE LONG, THE TIME SPENT TRAVELING HAS GIVEN HIM AND THE FAMILY AN UNBEATABLE OPPORTUNITY TO DISCOVER NEW AND INTERESTING CITIES. The family's main base is an apartment in fashionable Soho, which is shown on pages 192-7, but they have recently bought a property in Bellport, Suffolk County, on Long Island. This beautiful, trim house made from shingle is featured first.

Bellport is a coastal village and only a short drive from the city, but it is miles away in terms of the peace it brings from the pace of urban life. There is nothing more life affirming than waking up in the morning and breathing in the untainted air. The small yard and pool help the family to make the best use of the wonderful summers. Bentley, the dog, loves it here just as much as they do after all the constraints of the city. I WAS STRUCK BY HOW WELL DESIGNED AND PLANNED THIS HOUSE IS, MAKING WEEKEND BREAKS RELAXING RATHER THAN CREATING MORE WORK. IT HAS BEEN PAINTED WHITE THROUGHOUT WITH A DISTINCTIVE MONOCHROME PALETTE, and bold splashes of dark brown and black in the art and some of the furniture.

Plain white bed linen complements the sunny bedroom perfectly, helping to create a soft and relaxing environment. A small black vintage lamp sits on the curved white chest, alongside a tree ornament with delicate flowers found in a Long Island antique store. Sprayed with white paint, it adds to the cohesion of the room. Another gray-on-white abstract painting hangs above.

◄─◄ Spraying empty picture frames
and relief-work white unites the
display and makes for an original
wall treatment opposite the bed in
Joe's room.

White walls, the lower half paneled
in wood, establish a peaceful
background in the bathroom, while
the old tin can holding toiletries and
the bamboo-style frame of the **1940s**
French mirror introduce subdued
color for added interest. The old,
white-painted table is given a shot
of glamour with a crystal drawer pull.

A simple table setting on this raw wood table extends a compelling invitation to dine. Both the table and the benches are made of recycled wood from soaring water towers. Black metal-mesh chairs by Russell Woodard supplement the seating. The oil painting to the right is by friend and artist Rainer Andreesen, and depicts Diana's father in the late 1930s.

Each piece on this table is decorative as well as practical. The white china and small glass plates, the vintage crystal pot of preserves, and the stack of white linen napkins tied with string look striking against the raw table. Nature plays a part, too, with a huge chunk of wood used as a bread container and a dried hydrangea.

Presentation and meticulous attention to detail make dining in this space very special

A focused selection of decorative objects—an ornate Victorian tureen, with molded ceramic flowers on the lid, glass domes of varying sizes containing ceramic birds, and a carved marble cross—gathered on top of the small console table in the dining room creates a well-balanced display. Hanging above the table is a moody etching by Andrew Dalton.

The decorating throughout is sleek and consistent, with the focus on brilliant white paintwork. This gives a fresh, bright appeal-when the sun is shining, it is actually quite startling. DIANA IS EXTREMELY CREATIVE, AND HAS A NATURAL ABILITY TO DEVISE SIMPLE AND CLEVER DECORATING IDEAS. She has collected many retro vases and objects, which she has skillfully sprayed in matte black or white paint, creating striking monochrome vignettes, to give the home a focused look. Presentation is of utmost importance. When setting the table, for example, she takes great care with the overall look and color balance.

This is the dining room seen at a different angle, looking from the kitchen. In this pared-down space, the vintage white French armoire, home to all the beautiful ceramics and sets of china, catches the eye, its beveled mirror front reflecting the white Venetian blinds. In direct contrast, the table is set with black accessories, creating a more dramatic effect as the natural light fades and the hanging industrial lamp in the corner gives a warm glow.

The middle room in this house is bold and dramatic, with a huge piece of abstract art painted by Jessica Langton setting the tone. The white leather Barcelona chair and the brown cowhide rug make a sensitive addition to the design of the space. The wonderful brown, slatted, mid-20th-century chair, picked up at a garage sale for a modest amount, has turned out to be a significant find—it is an early **1970s** design by Brazilian designer Jorge Zalszupin.

Diana has decorated and furnished this home with meticulous care and a distinctive style. Every tiny detail is important to her, and SHE IS RIGHT TO CARE BECAUSE THE OVERALL EFFECT IS BEAUTIFUL. I WAS SO IMPRESSED that I immediately wanted to copy her ideas! The couple own some impressive pieces of art, many painted for them by friends with colors suited to the house. AS WITH SO MANY OF MY FAVORITE HOMES, MODERN, ICONIC DESIGNS ARE MIXED HERE VERY CLEVERLY WITH VINTAGE FINDS AND COMMISSIONED ART.

↑ This room, known to the family as the den, is where everyone
↑ relaxes and watches TV. It's a comfortable mix of retro and
modern. The brown sofa, with cushions covered in a 1950s
green splash fabric, add a subtle hint of color. Spotlighting
the rich brown walls is a modern, black, angled floor lamp.
The antler lamp was made by their friend Liddy Holt.

↑ The dark, painted walls are in contrast to the
↑ white in the rest of the house, giving the den a
cozy feel. A color palette of predominantly brown
and cream for the furniture enhances the effect.
Above the Danish Modern folding chair by Ebert
Wells hangs an abstract painting by Andrew Egan.

The open-plan living area in their Manhattan home, with the kitchen in the background, is utterly compelling. A large mirror is suspended from the ceiling, bouncing back natural light from the window opposite into the room. Reflected in it, you can see the George Nelson floor lamp on its tripod legs. The walls have been taken back to the raw brick and painted white, a striking contrast against the dark wood polished floorboards, lightening the space even further. A gas fire burns in the open fireplace, bringing a warm glow to this seductively light apartment.

↑ Glass bricks above the Saarinen dining table increase the feeling of light. The chairs are a mix of Norman Cherner and a vintage Kodawood clam-shell design found in California (as was the mid-century bench below the art). Beautifully turned wooden candlesticks by Liddy Holt are the sole decorative addition when the table is not in use. The wall of art is made up of a selection of vintage finds, precious personal art, and pictures painted by good friends.

➥ A wider-angle picture of the kitchen reveals clearly just how beautiful and stylish this apartment is.

Bringing even more natural light into the apartment are the long sash windows that look out over a light well. The dark colors of the furniture—the mid-20th-century leather sofa, the glossy black coffee table, and the early 1960s Harvey Probber velvet club chair —are offset to perfection by the white-painted brick walls. The George Nelson floor lamp emits a golden glow to the space. Just one piece of wall art— a Martyn Thompson photograph—is all that's needed to decorate this side of the apartment.

A net of pea lights has been strung across the three windows, giving the space a magical quality, as well as providing some privacy. The wooden struts to the sides are supports for the bedrooms above.

MODERN INDUSTRIALISTS 5

This is a term that has been bandied about frequently in the last few years. We have seen a real increase in the home of recycled, reused, or restored furniture, often originally from factories and other places of manual work. Here, you will see metal cabinets from laboratories, stripped back to the raw material, for holding china and glass; old carts, once wheeled around shoe factories, for storing towels in a bedroom; cupboards built from old floorboards; and large factory lamps in a domestic kitchen. The look is smart and, when mixed with textiles and art, not overly masculine. It becomes thoroughly modern and unique.

COOL COUPLE, SINGLE VISION

Kit Li-Perry and her husband Max live with their two children, Kai and Bay, in the Prospect Park South neighborhood of Brooklyn, New York. A BUSY WORKING COUPLE, THEY BOTH COMMUTE INTO THE CITY FOR THEIR WORK IN THE FASHION INDUSTRY. LIVING IN BROOKLYN IS FAIRLY NEW FOR THE FAMILY—THIS IS THEIR THIRD HOME IN THREE YEARS AFTER FIRST MOVING FROM LONDON TO PHILADELPHIA—but Kai and Bay seem perfectly unfazed by these adventures brought about by their parents' work. They thrive on new surroundings and enjoy making new friends.

THEIR LIGHT-FILLED AND COMFORTABLE HOUSE IS A FINE EXAMPLE OF LATE VICTORIAN ARCHITECTURE, SPACIOUS WITH PANELED WALLS, AN ABUNDANCE OF SASH WINDOWS, AND UNFUSSY DECORATIVE DETAILS, SUCH AS CORNICES AND PANELED DOORS. Kit and Max have a great love of industrial furniture and iconic design, and the house, being more than one hundred years old, is an unlikely although exceptional showcase for more contemporary pieces. Outdoors, the backyard, complete with a deck and fishpond, offers plenty of space for the children to play and for enjoying barbecues during the long summers.

Many of the important pieces in this home have traveled with the family on their journeys. THERE IS FURNITURE THAT MAX HAS COLLECTED FROM HIS TIME WORKING WITH A FRIEND IN LONDON, RESTORING AND RECYCLING WONDERFUL INDIVIDUAL PIECES. Kit's involvement with the world of interiors in the UK has resulted in treasures that simply have a rare and individual quality. Mixed in with all of these things are gifts from friends.

↑, ◄ In the dining room, the spider-like pendant light, Dear Ingo by Moooi, makes a powerful statement above the table made from a solid piece of wood and sitting on iron legs. Eames chairs by Vitra and the two iconic Wishbone chairs complement it perfectly. Softening the space is the rainbow rug by West Elm, while an old London bus sign adds a nostalgic note. The brushed-steel cabinet is filled with precious items collected on their travels.

The couple's love of iconic design, particularly from the mid-20th century, is on show in every room of the house, particularly the dining room. The detail picture on the left is a perfect example of their ability to mix various periods and materials together. BEHIND THE EAMES CHAIRS AT THE DINING TABLE, THE LONG SIDEBOARD, TYPICAL OF THE 1960S, COMPLEMENTS THE VICTORIAN WOOD PANELING BEHIND. THE UNIQUE COLLECTION OF ITEMS MADE FROM METAL, CHINA, AND WOOD ON TOP, COLLECTED OR RESTORED BY MAX AND KIT, PULLS THE WHOLE SCHEME TOGETHER. Evidence of the family's time spent in London is all around, with bus destination signs in the dining room and sitting room being particularly nostalgic reminders. Overall, the decorating style is subtle and muted but, here and there, pops of color brighten things up, as with the cushions on the 1960s sofa.

◄━ The original wall paneling and the mid-20th-century sideboard are perfect partners. Displayed on top are a number of special items with emotional significance. The two lamps have been remodeled from old lamp parts, while the radio has been made entirely from rosewood. All are in working order. The two pieces of pottery are from the 1960s.

↑ The mid-century sofa, with its colorful cushions, and the London bus sign compound the retro feel of the sitting room.

A simple but bold decorating style gives a real urban quality to this period house

▲ Even in Kit and Max's simply designed bedroom, with its dark brown walls echoing the paneling of the downstairs rooms and the contrasting white wood trim, there is an industrial feel. A wooden and metal cart acts as functional storage for towels and toiletries. Above the bed hangs a Le Klint pendant light.

In addition to the bedrooms and bathrooms on the first floor, there is a tiny room with a hand basin, just visible behind the open door in the photograph above—an unexpected design feature of this quirky Victorian house. It connects the master bedroom to the upstairs living room, where Kit and Max like to relax and enjoy a game of backgammon while the children sleep in their adjoining rooms. EVEN IN THE BEDROOMS, THE COUPLE HAVE CONTINUED WITH THEIR SIMPLE BUT BOLD APPROACH TO DECORATING, AND GIVEN A REAL URBAN QUALITY TO THE HOUSE, BRINGING IT BANG UP TO DATE.

←◄ Vintage brushed-steel filing cabinets are used to hold the small television and telephone.

←◄ An original **1930s** Anglepoise lamp, restored to working order, sits on top of the tall cabinet made from different pieces of recycled wood. White blinds filter the light through this dark but well-put-together room.

↑ A stool, possibly once used in a light industrial space during the **1930s**, has been cleverly converted into a bedside table. The lamp on top, restored and recycled from original pieces, adds a solitary splash of color.

CREATIVE PARTNERSHIP

◄ Uniformly spaced and in matching unobtrusive frames, Rick's black-and-white photographs of Molly, the couple's other daughter, and Darcy, from when they were growing up in New York, make a sleek and well-thought-out display above the recycled, dark-stained sideboard. On top, vintage glass decanters and jars form part of a carefully curated selection of objects collected over the years.

➤ Of huge interest to Alfie, a vintage, brushed-steel office cabinet doubles up as handsome storage and a display surface. Rick took the photograph above of a building reflected in a puddle.

Rick Haylor, a photographer, and his business partner wife Debra live and work together in this brownstone in Fort Greene, a leafy part of Brooklyn, New York. Sharing the home is their 19-year-old daughter Darcy, plus Alfie, the dog. The British couple made the decision to leave Manhattan a few years ago, to put down their roots in this bustling neighborhood, which is awash with small independent restaurants and stores, and has a park close by for walking Alfie. THERE IS A CONSTANT STREAM OF LIKE-MINDED FRIENDS OF ALL NATIONALITIES IN AND OUT OF THEIR STYLISH HOME, ADDING TO THE AMAZINGLY CREATIVE AND ENERGETIC ATMOSPHERE THAT ALREADY EXISTS. What I particularly like about this home is the way in which Rick and Debra have merged two distinct styles, combining the original features of their

period house with brushed steel and an industrial look from another decade entirely.

THIS LARGE THROUGH-ROOM IS THE FOCAL POINT FOR FAMILY DINING AS WELL AS ENTERTAINING. THE VINTAGE BRUSHED-STEEL TABLE, CHAIRS, AND GLAZED CABINET GIVE AN URBAN, INDUSTRIAL FEEL, but this is offset by the ceramic pitcher of flowers and glassware, creating a distinctive yet relaxed dining area. The beautiful parquet floors are original to the house and also help to soften the space. On the opposite side of the room is the marble fireplace, also original, with various decorative objects jostling for space on top.

◄━ﬤ **A** brushed-steel table and matching curved-back chairs, which might once have belonged in a small factory or office, now have pride of place in this contemporary home. **Vinyl**-coated vintage office chairs introduce a softer and eclectic feel to this cool and sophisticated space.

▲ The ornate marble mantel shelf ꓕ is jam-packed with favored decorative objects, from white ornamental vases of various shapes and sizes to a stuffed bird and vintage glass domes covering all manner of eclectic treasures. Adding a vibrant splash of color is an arrangement of dried hydrangeas in their autumnal green livery. Behind, highlighting this carefully considered display, is a round mosaic mirror, its beveled edges twinkling with reflections.

STYLE FUSION IN A CALM URBAN SPACE

◄━ Contrasting styles appear side by side in every room. In the living space, the original wooden fireplace is the elegant showcase for a piece of spray-painted graffiti art by the street artist duo "Best Ever." A vintage tailor's dummy displays a **1930s** pearly king coat, ceremonial garb for London street traders. Favorite items displayed on the leaning shelf include a diverse collection of books, a stuffed owl in flight, and a small glass dome protecting a neatly folded dollar bill in the shape of a ring. Bradley gave this to Caitlin in New York when he proposed, as a substitute until they chose the real thing together.

▲ A tiny chair displays a jumble of vintage wooden letters, alongside a pair of Bradley's well-loved sneakers.

Trained as an interior designer, Caitlin McCann works as a retail interiors and textiles buyer. She loves fine fabrics and beautiful things, and has an incredible eye for detail. In contrast, her husband Bradley Ridge, a restaurant owner, is an avid collector of street art and urban graphics. NO ONE COULD POSSIBLY HAVE PREDICTED WHAT KIND OF HOME THEIR WILDLY DIVERGENT TASTES WOULD CREATE, EXCEPT THAT IT WOULD BE UNIQUE. Caitlin and Bradley have made a home where their styles have been merged with great integrity. It is warm, tranquil, and sensual but with a sharp urban edge. For me, it is very special when this sort of thing happens and a one-off is produced in a truly organic, non-formulaic way.

THE PAIR SPENT A LONG TIME LOOKING FOR JUST THE RIGHT PLACE TO CALL HOME AND EVENTUALLY FOUND THIS PERIOD PROPERTY IN STREATHAM, SOUTHWEST LONDON. They both knew immediately that it was right for them—Bradley's restaurant, where they had also met, was in Streatham, after all—and the journey of making a home began.

◄━ This wider view of the living space shown on the two previous pages reveals even more of the couple's vintage finds and the apparently effortless way they have been put together. Sheepskin throws add a bohemian touch to the desk chair and the black Barcelona chair with the ottoman footrest. A small copper jug containing the creamiest of roses sits on the small glass table with its decorative supports in a golden wheat design. Casting atmospheric shadows over the wall is a **1960**s Chrome Pistillo lamp, a funky contrast to the vintage decorative crystal chandelier.

These two shelves house some remarkable and very individual pieces of art from different eras, highlighting the couple's very different styles and interests. Top row, from left to right: a plaque by the British urban graffiti artist Stik of his signature stick man; mounted antique printing blocks; etchings of a dove and a more abstract bird; and an antique letter "R." Bottom row: mounted vintage gloves; an antique gilt frame; a vintage oil painting; and a mixed media framed pope by the French street artist Dran.

EVERY FRIDAY

STREATHAM: PAIR SNUB TV SHOW'S £240K BANKSY

Art is a quick and easy way to transform the feel of a space as well as speaking volumes about its owner

▲▲ Slatted shutters fill the bay windows of this comfortable living space, filtering light and allowing privacy. Two artworks on the wall—another Dran piece, "Monkey at Work," by the window, and the David Bailey photographic print, "King of Clubs"—hint at a more subversive, humorous approach to decoration than would otherwise be suggested by the modern, cream corner sofa unit, pouffe, and antique chairs.

Caitlin and I have worked together for many years and I'VE LOST COUNT OF THE NUMBER OF INTERIORS SHOWS AROUND THE WORLD THAT WE HAVE VISITED, sourcing remarkable things for the store. But THE VISITS HAVE ALSO GIVEN US A FANTASTIC BACK CATALOG OF IDEAS TO STORE AWAY FOR WHENEVER WE DECORATE OUR OWN HOMES. I'm aware of what makes Caitlin tick and I know what it must have taken for her to source every piece here-she will have not

left anything to chance. SHE HAS A VERY CLEAR UNDERSTANDING OF WHAT SHE WANTS AND, INDEED, WANTS TO LIVE WITH, from the paint color for the walls to the finish of the floorboards. Bradley, too, shares a passion for getting it right, and his mark is just as apparent. Both of them had decorated their own homes previously, and the inevitable compromise that had to be reached for this shared home must have been an enormous challenge.

◄━◄ A modern BTC white light hangs in the spare room. Reflected in the armoire's beveled mirror door is an artist's proof print of Nola by the British street artist Banksy. This vignette shows yet another example of the unexpected synergy created between vintage and contemporary: a stunning piece of French furniture with modern lighting and street art.

▷━► A tall, brushed-steel cabinet houses some of Caitlin and Bradley's favorite china and glass, including Caitlin's grandmother's gold Royal Worcester coffee set. The London bus destination sign above is a humorous and very meaningful addition.

Caitlin's retail training has given her great insight into how objects are made and what makes them of great quality, FROM THE FINEST CASHMERE THROW TO A SIMPLE LINEN DISHTOWEL. SHE ALSO KNOWS WHERE IN THE WORLD THE BEST EXAMPLES OF ALL THESE THINGS CAN BE FOUND. Bradley, meanwhile, has an unbridled passion for urban art, and his quest to source the exact pieces he wants is admirable-he even used a graffiti artist to create a piece of art when he proposed to Caitlin!

STREATHAM VIA TOOTING

Traditional meets urban with a cabinet of precious china and a vintage London bus destination sign

THE ARCHIVIST

6

Living a life in and around a vast archive is not something that most people would ever have the chance to do. But if you are lucky enough to be able to, like Barnaba Fornasetti who is featured here, what a thrill each day must bring. The archive and its preservation is a huge responsibility in itself, but Barnaba has very cleverly used it to his advantage and made it an intrinsic part of how he lives. To interpret such a decorating style in your own home would involve researching and finding designs or decorations from a favorite period or designer/artist and bringing them to life in whatever way feels right.

THE SKILLFUL VISIONARY

Barnaba is the son of Piero Fornasetti, one of Italy's most talented artists, sculptors, and interior decorators. Based IN CENTRAL MILAN, BARNABA MANAGES HIS FATHER'S VAST ARCHIVE AND CONTINUES TO PRODUCE AND REVIVE FORNASETTI DESIGNS WITH GREAT FLAIR AND INTEGRITY, MAKING THEM AS COLLECTIBLE AND DESIRABLE AS EVER. At the helm of the company and its creative heart, Barnaba is the custodian of his father's legacy. He lives in his father's house, right in amongst the archive, in a wonderfully magical and eclectic space. Barnaba hosts the most sensational parties, endlessly entertains, and enjoys sharing the unique beauty of his home.

Barnaba's home is a cornucopia of rare and original works from his father which he has used to create A HOME OF OUTSTANDING ORIGINALITY AND BEAUTY. HE RE-WORKS OLD ART AND GIVES IT A MODERN TWIST, or simply mixes unique one-offs with his current collections.

◄◄ The kitchen is a new extension which has been added to the original house. Floor-to-ceiling windows allow breathtaking views of the garden. Hanging majestically above the table is a spectacular glass chandelier from Murano. The table, laid by Barnaba, displays the most beautiful Fornasetti porcelain.

➤➤ On close inspection, you will see a signature Fornasetti artwork of newspaper print covered in butterflies on every surface, from floor tiles to the chairs and across the surface of the table. This creates a slightly surreal atmosphere, almost like a hothouse—a typically whimsical Fornasetti style.

↑, ▷▶ Barnaba loves music of all kinds, from classical to jazz and modern, and owns literally thousands of CDs and vinyl albums. They fill an entire wall of specially designed fitted shelving in this library. Other shelves are full to the brim with books, all of them logged by theme, covering subjects from Japanese architecture to plants and flowers, and everything in between. The 1960s sofa and two chairs, with their fake bamboo frames, are decorated with a selection of Fornasetti printed cushions. A porcelain cat—there are many, in different sizes, all over the house—has made itself at home on the "bamboo" coffee table.

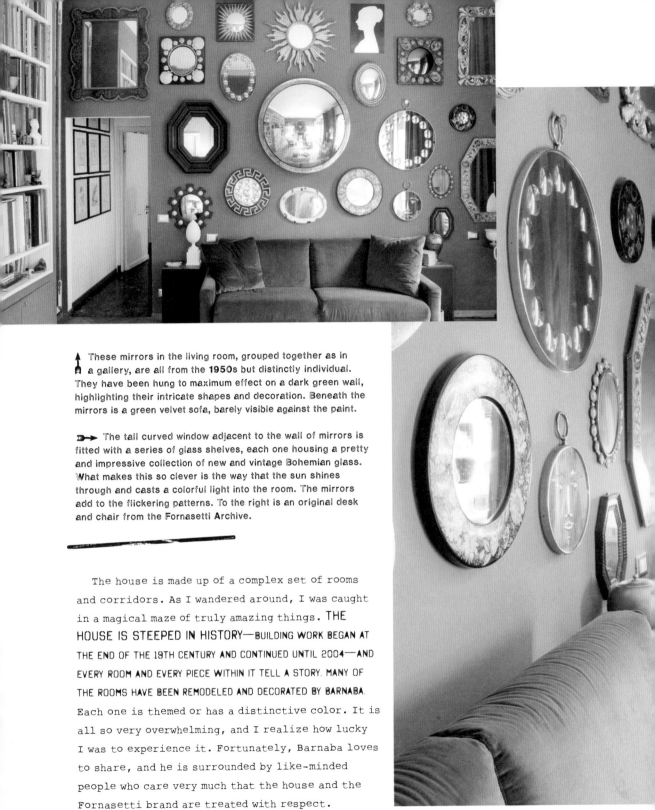

↑ These mirrors in the living room, grouped together as in a gallery, are all from the **1950**s but distinctly individual. They have been hung to maximum effect on a dark green wall, highlighting their intricate shapes and decoration. Beneath the mirrors is a green velvet sofa, barely visible against the paint.

➡ The tall curved window adjacent to the wall of mirrors is fitted with a series of glass shelves, each one housing a pretty and impressive collection of new and vintage Bohemian glass. What makes this so clever is the way that the sun shines through and casts a colorful light into the room. The mirrors add to the flickering patterns. To the right is an original desk and chair from the Fornasetti Archive.

The house is made up of a complex set of rooms and corridors. As I wandered around, I was caught in a magical maze of truly amazing things. THE HOUSE IS STEEPED IN HISTORY—BUILDING WORK BEGAN AT THE END OF THE 19TH CENTURY AND CONTINUED UNTIL 2004—AND EVERY ROOM AND EVERY PIECE WITHIN IT TELL A STORY. MANY OF THE ROOMS HAVE BEEN REMODELED AND DECORATED BY BARNABA. Each one is themed or has a distinctive color. It is all so very overwhelming, and I realize how lucky I was to experience it. Fortunately, Barnaba loves to share, and he is surrounded by like-minded people who care very much that the house and the Fornasetti brand are treated with respect.

The dark green walls in this sitting room are a perfect backdrop when showcasing so much art and diverse decoration. The 17th-century octagonal mirror above the marble fireplace makes a bold statement, unlike the two white leather Chesterfields from another age, which are very subdued in comparison. The original **Piero Fornasetti** drum shades on tall stands add to the perfect balance of the room. Symmetry is very obvious here, which is vital when using so many styles and patterns.

1001 DISCHI

◄▬ This first-floor studio is where Barnaba used to work. Piero's design tools are still hanging in the same place they always used to, above the "Riga e Squadra" desk that Barnaba designed. What strikes me is how well ordered and tidy everything is, how precious and well cared for. There is so much to look at in this photograph. The plaster hand holding a pencil draws the eye first, and this is to me almost a statement of what the room was used for. It is based on the hand of David in the statue by Michelangelo, and is reminiscent of the Fornasetti logo, which depicts a hand holding a pencil. A religious icon by the staircase sits next to a vintage Fornasetti butterfly obelisk lamp. Beneath, a pair of ceramic soldiers' boots is used to hold long paintbrushes. Keeping an eye on you as you climb the stairs to the study above is a quirky metal cat, given to Barnaba as a gift by its creator, artist Fabius Tita. All these pieces are clear expressions of Barnaba's playful sense of humor.

This is truly an exceptional house but it is very difficult
to talk about the decorating style, as there is not just
one. However, I do want to share with readers the sense of
history here and the unique quality of living in an archive.
PIERO'S STYLE AND GENIUS ARE EVIDENT EVERYWHERE YOU
LOOK. ON THE FIRST FLOOR, THERE ARE UMPTEEN FILES CONTAINING ARTICLES
OR CUTTINGS, ALL ARRANGED BY THEME AND CAREFULLY FILED AWAY FOR
FUTURE REFERENCE. The "Riga e Squadra" desk, designed and
used by Barnaba, displays all the tools of Piero's craft
(see pages 230-1). The arrangement of all the pieces in
the house, and the way in which everything is cared for,

↑, ▭▶ It must feel rather strange
sleeping in this red room, one of
the many bedrooms in the house.
Almost everything in it is red, from
the walls to the lampshade, and I am
told that every single book in the
house with a red cover has been
moved here—even the book titles all
contain the word "red"! The picture
of the dandyish fellow is one of
ten depicting the history of men's
clothes. Over the wooden sleigh bed
hangs an original convex mirror in
a gold frame.

is really impressive but it must be remembered that it's also essential for the longevity of the Fornasetti brand and the preservation of its past.

There are clever and inspiring vignettes all around, such as the window lined with glass shelves that display brightly colored Murano glassware (see pages 226~7) and through which the brilliant summer sun is reflected-no accident but created for maximum impact. Dark-colored walls set off precious mirrors, most of them original but some are Barnaba's "re-inventions."

THE HOUSE IS MUCH MORE THAN A REVERENTIAL LOOK AT THE PAST. BARNABA HAS USED HIS SKILL TO GIVE THIS FAMILY HOME A MODERN TWIST, BREATHING NEW LIFE THROUGH THE SPACE AND ALSO THROUGH THE ART AND THE ORIGINAL DESIGNS. There are literally thousands of these and, working with the best, he is slowly franchising certain imagery to specialist manufacturers. Their signature fragrance, Otto, uses ingredients found in and around the home, but it is the ceramic packaging, inspired by imagery from the archive, especially the Fornasetti "face," that is for many the most memorable. Cole & Son now offer amazing Fornasetti wallpaper, so there is no reason why you shouldn't re-create the look yourself.

↑ , ➡➡ The original Fornasetti mirror in the living room is from the **1950s** and very rare. It is also very beautiful and quite dramatic. Hanging above an original leopard-design cabinet and between the wall and large walnut wardrobe, it somehow manages to look rather subdued. The large round "Architettura" table displays two red ceramic dogs from the Fornasetti Archive. Beneath the red piano is a pouffe covered in fabric of an original design.

I AM SURE THAT ANYONE READING THIS BOOK WILL BE INSPIRED BY SOMETHING IN THIS HOUSE AND WANT TO TRY IT FOR THEMSELVES. An all-red room, with red walls, red textiles, even a red light might never have occurred to you, but seeing the one on pages 232–3 and appreciating its drama might just change all that! After all, it's fun borrowing ideas.

Most of the modern and new Fornasetti products are produced in the atelier in Milan. They are all rigorously created in limited editions and then signed by the craftsman. It is a thriving business, and Fornasetti creations are sold all over the world to the best retailers. The flagship retail store, also in Milan, is well worth a visit. Original pieces are loaned to

There is something to inspire everyone in this house

▼ Original Fornasetti designs
are slowly being licensed to
specialist manufacturers. In the
master bedroom, the walls have
been covered with a cloud design
wallpaper, produced by the British
company Cole & Son. Either side of
the **1950s** "Architettura" cabinet,
the elegant chairs, with their
exceptionally tall backs, are made
by Chiavari, Genova.

museums for exhibitions, so you may be lucky enough to experience Fornasetti design closer to home.

The bathroom has also been treated with the same uncompromising style. The Fornasetti "face" has been repeated in its many guises on the black bathroom tiles. It is dramatic to say the least. THE SHALLOW BLACK PORCELAIN BOWLS AND THE ORIGINAL CERAMIC ORNAMENTS AND BOWLS IN THE PATTERN, TOGETHER WITH THE CURTAIN AT THE WINDOW, MAKE A HUGE STATEMENT. The iconic, enigmatic face was created by Piero, taken from images of the opera singer Lina Cavalieri that he found in

↑ This striking bathroom is tiled completely in black, with different versions of the Fornasetti "face"— some surreal, some funny, all interesting—dotted here and there. The window has a curtain made from Fornasetti fabric, depicting the faces, and the tall porcelain jars and vases continue the theme. The shallow basins and the tub indicate that this is a functional bathroom, not just an incredible display.

a 19th-century French magazine, and reproduced in literally hundreds of guises, some surreal and some amusing, but all surprising.

MY VISIT TO BARNABA'S HOME WAS NOTHING SHORT OF A FANTASTIC ADVENTURE. I LOVED THE SENSE OF EXCITEMENT AT NOT KNOWING WHAT TREASURE I WOULD SEE NEXT. The team who work for Barnaba are incredibly well informed and all too willing to share their knowledge. They are also passionate about Fornasetti, and that is infectious. I can't wait to go back!

AUTHOR'S ACKNOWLEDGMENTS

I would like to thank Cindy Richards, Gillian Haslam, and Sally Powell from CICO Books for all their continued support and expertise in creating this book, Paul Tilby for yet again delivering an amazing layout, and Helen Ridge for her clever words and for keeping me on the straight and narrow when under pressure.

Andrew Wood—what can I say?! A great photographer, who has captured the perfect images for such a diverse cross-section of interesting homes. We have worked together on the last three books and they would not have happened or been so successful without him, so thank you. I look forward to the next three books! It has been so much fun.

To everyone who is featured in this book—you will know them all by now. They welcomed Andrew and I into their homes, nearly always at the weekend, and on many occasions fed us or plied us with coffee. They generously allowed us to rummage around, move things and tidy or reorganize—thank you so much. I have learnt so much and fed my insatiable appetite to look at new and interesting and, above all, original decorating and design ideas.

To Rosie, my daughter, once again for her unstinting support. To Rob Falconer, Louise Ames, and Sarah Smith—my work colleagues who I have driven mad most of the time.

And, finally, to Eddie, our new rescue dog, just because he makes us so happy.

For further information on the homeowners, please see their websites:

Patric & Christina Shaw:
  www.patricshawbeauty.com
Ornella Pisano: www.ercolehome.com
Gisela Garcia Escula: www.anthropologie.com
Paul Brewster & Shaun Clarkson:
  www.pitfieldlondon.com

Joel Bernstein: www.cocomaya.co.uk
Richard Nott: www.richardnott-artist.com
John Derian: www.johnderian.com
Debby Kuypers: www.rfkarchitects.co.uk
Rick & Debra Haylor: www.rickhaylor.com
Barnaba Fornasetti: www.fornasetti.com

BARNABA FORNASETTI

JOEL BERNSTEIN

GERALDINE

BETTY JACKSON & DAVID COHEN

DEBRA & RICK HAYLOR

CHRIST